GO
&Make
Disciples

D0061871

GO
&Make
Disciples

David H. C. Read

Abingdon/Nashville

Go . . . and Make Disciples

Copyright © 1978 by David H. C. Read

Library of Congress Cataloging in Publication Data

READ, DAVID HAXTON CARSWELL.
  Go . . . and make disciples.
  1. Evangelistic work—Addresses, essays, lectures. I. Title.
BV3795.R42   269'.2   78-1881

ISBN 0-687-14892-8

Scripture quotations noted NEB are from The New English
Bible. © the Delegates of the Oxford University Press and the
Syndics of the Cambridge University Press 1961, 1970.
Reprinted by permission.

MANUFACTURED BY THE PARTHENON PRESS AT
NASHVILLE, TENNESSEE, UNITED STATES OF AMERICA

In Memoriam
Jesse M. Bader
(1900-1963)

Contents

Preface

Evangelism is again in the news. Some are delighted; some are disgusted; some are frankly puzzled.

This book is chiefly addressed to those who are not quite sure what evangelism is; to those church members who feel they ought to believe in it but are not sure that they do; and to non-members who resent what looks like Christian aggression in an age of religious pluralism.

I am grateful to Dr. K. R. Bowes, principal of the College of the Bible in Melbourne, for the invitation to deliver what is here printed as the Jesse Bader Memorial lectures in June, 1976, and for the warm hospitality of Australian friends. It has also been stimulating to discuss these questions with my own church members and with friends who are members of other churches, or of none.

My secretary, Carolyn Mathis, deserves special thanks for expert assistance with the manuscript and patience with the author.

I

The Case Against Evangelism

Evangelism is a subject about which most people would seem to have made up their minds. Those who are convinced that being a Christian carries an obligation to pass on the good news, to spread the gospel to others near and far, will not feel the need for any further argument or want to have some loquacious clergyman complicating what is for them a very simple issue. On the other hand, the large numbers for whom "evangelism" is an ugly word with undertones of emotionalism and extremism (not to mention bigotry, arrogance, fanaticism, and fraud) are not in the market for any book with this word on the cover. So who needs it? Neither, it seems, the Christian who is already an evangelist at heart, nor the one inside or outside the church who is totally opposed to what is thought of as "interfering with other people's religion" and who is deeply suspicious of the techniques and trappings of mass evangelism. Thus we find that most books on the subject assume a certain preliminary piety in the reader, an agreement that evangelism is something we should be doing, and perhaps a guilty conscience that we are not. They, therefore, tend to be mildly theological stimuli for the faithful, or, even more common in this country, "How-to" books filled with formulas and techniques for the saving of souls and the expansion of the churches. (A recent book of this kind presented me with the somewhat unhelpful recommendation that the first step in successful evangelism is to make sure that your church has a parking lot for several thousand cars.)

Since this analysis seems to leave this book without an audience, let me explain what prompts me to raise the question at this point in eternity (the church, we should remember, doesn't just deal with points in time). I sense a subtle change in the popular response to the sound of the word "evangelism." There are signs that it no longer elicits a knee-jerk reaction among either its friends or enemies, and there is a new willingness to ask what it really means. I hope I am addressing those who, whatever their prejudices may have been, are ready to ask again what is meant by this peculiar activity of the church and the individual Christian, what its origin and history have been, and how it fits into our picture of life in the last quarter of the twentieth century.

For the last hundred years in this country, the word "evangelism" has been colored by the image of the mass-meeting at which an appeal is made for a decision for Christ. Until quite recently this was what evangelism meant for millions, whether they were for it or against it. No matter what the dictionary or the textbooks said, this concept was rooted in the popular mind, and you were for or against evangelism according to your feelings about the kind of campaign associated at its inception with Moody and Sankey and now, almost inevitably, with Billy Graham, and perhaps with some much less reputable characters in between. Without passing any judgment on the legitimacy or the effectiveness of such campaigns at this point, we ought to note that this particlar phenomenon is a comparatively recent invention in the two-thousand-year history of the church. We must recognize that evangelism is not just the name for one particular method of declaring the gospel of Christ but is something rooted in the life of the church from New Testament times, which has taken many forms at different times in different parts of the world.

Shaking loose from this narrow and limited concept of evangelism has meant a renewed concern with its basic meaning. In recent years evangelism has ceased to be the neglected and somewhat disreputable step-sister in the typical mainline churches. The ecclesiastical snobbery that relegated this kind of thing to the fundamentalist fringe or the storefront sects, has happily almost disappeared; and assemblies and conventions, bishops and bureaucrats, as well as eminent theologians, have been giving the subject their vigorous attention. Local churches that had channeled any enthusiasm for evangelism into the safe haven of an appropriate committee suddenly began to realize that the propagation of the gospel is the business of the entire congregation. The younger generation, more clear-eyed about the contemporary situation of the church in a secularized society, has added its excitement to the growing concern. Staid church members, and even our friendly and somewhat cynical observers, are beginning to see that evangelism is a mighty word that covers far more than hitting the sawdust trail or being asked embarrassing questions about the state of one's soul.

At the same time here have been some fascinating rumblings from the camp of the conservatives in the church who have always given unquestioning support to evangelistic efforts of all kinds. Not only have the methods of the modern mass meeting with its techniques and stereotypes been questioned, but the theology behind the conventional appeals for decision has been exposed to criticism on scriptural grounds. Some have indicated their uneasiness with an evangelism that puts all the emphasis on human decision and reckons little with the grace of God. The latent Calvinism in our Christian tradition is uneasy with a popular evangelical theology that neglects the doctrine of divine election and has little to say about the covenant relationship of the baptized with their God. Some are quick to smell out the heresy of Pelagianism. (Pelagius was the fourth-century theologian who taught that our salvation depended on human actions as well as God's.) It is pointed out that much modern evangelism with its stress on the moment of conversion, its use of decision cards, its use of standardized questions and answers, its deliberate employment of psychological pressures and emotion arousing techniques, has strayed far from the New Testament. So even among the ranks of the orthodox some serious rethinking is going on, and evangelism is no longer automatically acceptable in its popular, twentieth-century form.

Out of this ferment in all sections of the church, there may well come a new wave of understanding and enthusiasm for the propagation of the gospel. What we are exploring is an extraordinary convergence of varieties of Christian theology and churchmanship on the task of evangelism—in the original (scriptural) sense of the word. What used to be called broad church, high church, and low church are at one in seeking new ways and new power to present the gospel to the indifferent and the unbelievers. The World Council of Churches set evangelism at the center of the Nairobi Assembly with its slogan Jesus Christ Frees and Unites. (The best ecumenical thinking has always based the search for Christian unity on the words of Jesus' prayer in the 17th chapter of John: "that they also may be one in us . . . so *that the world may believe* that thou has sent me.") The Pope has repeatedly summoned the faithful to greater energy and dedication in proclaiming the gospel in a materialist age. Theologians of every stripe have been contributing their insights to the meaning and purpose of evangelism. Clearly it is being impressed on the church in this age of revolution that without the dynamics of evangelism history will pass us by leaving a vestigial body of Christians to wither on the vine.

Yet still there is a hesitancy among the ranks of church members and a growing opposition among non-Christians to what appears to them to be a threatening militancy on the part of the Christian church. This was illustrated not long ago in the United States by the launching of an evangelistic campaign on a national scale entitled "Key '73". Its avowed aim was the winning of converts to Jesus Christ in every part of the country. At the height of its impact, I asked a representative group of our church members to indicate if they had heard of it, and only a few indicated that they even knew the name. Yet during that same period, I was asked about the campaign by several rabbis who said that their own people were disturbed and alarmed by what seemed an aggressive intention on the part of the Christian church to win converts. What lies behind this coolness on the part of many Christians and the growing resentment on the part of adherents of other faiths or of none? In an attempt to answer this question I will try to interpret the reasoning behind the suspicion and dislike that one encounters both inside and outside the churches. To some extent the rest of this book will be addressed to the task of answering the case against evangelism, but it is well to begin by analyzing these arguments and sorting out the frivolous from the serious. I hope that I shall not put the case against evangelism so cogently that some will lay down the book after the first chapter thoroughly reinforced in their prejudices.

Criticism of evangelism falls roughly into one of two categories: what is expressed is either a revulsion from certain *methods* of evangelism or a fundamental, objection to the *concept* itself. The latter is by far the most serious criticism to be answered, but the former looms large in the popular mind.

It is not difficult to build up a superficial case against evangelism by listing certain methods that have been used, particularly in the last hundred years, and exposing them to serious criticism, if not to ridicule and contempt.

(1) First, there is the distaste of the intellectual for anything that falls into the category of mass hysteria. Christian evangelism is regarded as just one other example of the manipulation of large crowds by dynamic oratory and elaborate staging, and a parallel is drawn between a vast evangelistic meeting in which a crowd is swayed by a magnetic speaker and rousing hymns, and, let us say, a rally at Nürnberg addressed by the late Adolf Hitler. There are those who shudder at any spectacle of mass-enthusiasm, even when their favorite candidate is getting nominated at a party convention, and they are revolted by the thought of a religion attempting to sell itself to the public by such methods. Even those who are themselves believers may feel strongly that this kind of evangelism debases what they hold to be sacred and have even been known to make uncharitable references to "casting pearls before swine." What this revulsion for evangelism implies is really a social rather than a theological

objection. Such a parading of religious feeling is felt to be in bad taste.

(2) This slightly snobbish aspect of a case against evangelism is, of course, reinforced by what you might call the seamy side of evangelistic activity. The popular evangelist, with the notable exception of Billy Graham, has not had a good press. The sad fact is that there have been notorious eccentrics, money-makers, and even crooks in the business of evangelism; and the novelists and filmmakers have not been slow to capitalize on their stories. Commercialized religion has been with us since at least the days of the Hebrew prophets, who had much to say on the subject. It was highlighted in the cleansing of the Temple precincts by Jesus. Rogues who play on the emotions of the gullible are, of course, operative in every area of life—in politics, in charitable activities, in the arts, and in business—but we find the religious charlatan to be particularly detestable. He is also, incidentally, the easiest to caricature, and an entire generation almost closed the case against evangelism on the evidence of the fictional character known as Elmer Gantry in the novel by that name by Sinclair Lewis. Say "evangelist" to a certain kind of person, and it is the image of Elmer Gantry that springs to his mind. So away with this gimmickery, hoopla, vulgarity, and commericalism, if that's what you mean by evangelism. As Wordsworth put it, "Great God! I'd rather be a pagan suckled in a creed outworn. . . . "

(3) But it's not only against the mass-meeting type of

evangelism that a damning indictment can be drawn. One of the strongest objections felt by the average man or woman is to the kind of nosy, offensive, or embarrassing intrusion into one's privacy that can go by the name of "personal evangelism." Even in these days of the ubiquitous questionnaire, most of us intensely resent being asked intimate questions about our personal religious beliefs, particularly by total strangers. Here again, another stereotype is rooted in the popular mind: a Christian who believes in evangelism is under a compulsion to accost all and sundry with the question, "Are you saved?" The question here is more than one of courtesy or good taste; it is a protest that no one has a right to demand to be shown what we may well believe to be our own private holy of holies. The case against evangelism of this type is so strong that many are prepared to rebuff every attempt to discuss religion.

There is a story about a lady in Edinburgh who was resolutely opposed to this form of evangelism. One Sunday evening she was waiting for a streetcar at the Mound, a location used by orators of various kinds and in particular at that time by a certain well-known evangelist. The meeting had just finished, and to her horror she saw that the evangelist was coming straight in her direction. She gathered her strength and had her answer ready. So when the poor man accosted her and said, "Excuse me, madam, but does the Number 6 car go to Marchmont?" she snapped back, "That's a matter between me and my God!"

(4) An even stronger case can be made against the

more violent forms of evangelism on the basis of the psychological damage that can result from crude appeals to the emotions of fear and guilt. Recently a young college professor told me a horrifying story of his own experience at the age of six. He had been dragged to the front row of an evangelistic meeting in a small town. At the close of his address the speaker made his appeal. At one point, looking straight at the little boy, he shouted: "If you don't come down here and accept Christ as your Savior, you'll burn in hell forever." I had often suspected that popular novelists have overdrawn this kind of preaching, but this man assured me that it actually happened. The miracle to me is that he was not lost forever to the Christian church.

Though I never experienced anything so rude and repulsive in my youth, I can remember being exposed on occasion to the kind of evangelism that played on the guilt feelings of the normal adolescent and used what now seems to me unwise pressures to elicit a confession of faith in Christ. Such evangelism can be accused of lack of respect for the individual personality, ignorance of the dangers of premature and enforced decisions, and the sacrifice of Christian love to the desire for spectacular conversions.

(5) Then, of course, there is the charge that evangelism is just another name for proselytism—the consuming desire to bring others, at all costs, into our particular religious fold. The strongest criticism of this type of evangelism I have ever heard came from a young man who was obviously revolted by this

narrow-minded crusade to corral everyone within reach. "You travel over sea and land to make one convert," he said; "and when you have won him he is twice as fit for hell as you are yourselves." It may come as a surprise to some to learn that the young man in question was Jesus of Nazareth, the same Jesus who said, "Go forth therefore and make all nations my disciples." Clearly if evangelism means proselytizing, the case against it is closed for Christians as well as non-Christians.

(6) There should perhaps be added a number of more or less frivolous objections to evangelists as a class and to the effects of certain kinds of evangelistic campaigns. Those who declare themselves against evangelism are often influenced by a picture they have developed of the starry-eyed enthusiast whose bubbling high spirits seem something less than human, and who exudes the kind of piety that sends a shudder down the spine. I remember once telling my mother that a certain evangelist had addressed us at morning chapel in my school. "Did he smile a lot?" she asked. And when I replied that he did, she said, "They always do," leaving me slightly puzzled. Such images of the evangelist can hardly be taken seriously as making a case against evangelism, but they loom large in the minds of those who are apt to say about any proposal to hold a mission or campaign designed to present the gospel to the unbeliever, "I don't believe in that kind of thing."

There is still a lingering belief among the older generation that evangelism should be frowned upon because it is based on the assumption that there are people around us who are not Christians and that is therefore vaguely insulting. When I offered a course of lectures many years ago designed to present the gospel to unbelievers, I advertized it as "Christianity for the Unconvinced." My father-in-law was horrified and indicated that he wouldn't be caught dead attending such a course.

Behind many of these objections, however, is the basic thought that evangelism of any kind is a somewhat embarrassing activity of which all respectable church members should steer clear. This opinion is reinforced by the fairly common impression that converts are a somewhat undesirable class of people. It is not difficult for most people to dig up examples of men or women who, in our eyes, were changed for the worse after they got religion, losing their sparkle and *joie de vivre* and acquiring a narrow and somewhat fanatical point of view. It is this that disturbs parents of offspring who are spiritually kidnapped by some evangelizing group and who undergo what looks like nothing less than brainwashing. There is also a healthy skepticism toward the convert, suspicion that his motives are less than religious, as in the case of the converted Jew who instead of not attending the synagogue, now stays away from church.

All this seems to add up to a pretty heavy indictment of the *methods* of evangelism that we have either experienced or read about (more often, I suspect, the latter). At this point I have no intention of answering them one by one. I pause simply to say that not one of these objections has any real bearing on the theory and practice of evangelism as evidenced in the New Testament or stands in the way of a genuine effort to spread the good news today and obey the Lord's command to make disciples. Much of this criticism has been earned by mistaken zeal and limited understanding of the true nature of evangelism and what we mean by "conversion." What I have listed doesn't amount to a case against evangelism but simply against certain evangelistic methods. It also, I suggest, depends heavily on prejudice and a very selective judgment of the fruits of such efforts to spread the gospel. For one phoney evangelist, I could show you a hundred who are genuine; and for one convert who has shriveled in the process, I could show you dozens who have found a more abundant life.

We have now to look at the really serious case against evangelism. And, like most important matters, it is basically theological. Many who are prepared to admit that evangelism should not be judged by the excesses, follies, or hypocrisies of its lunatic fringe (*corruptio optimi pessima*—"corruption of the best is the worst"—is a principle that applies here) have nevertheless a fundamental objection to the very concept of a religion attempting to expand by winning adherents from other faiths or from the ranks of unbelief. Their case against evangelism is that it presupposes a conviction of the superiority of one religious teaching over all others, hence it is arrogant, and it introduces an unnecessary tension in a society where it has been agreed that all religions have equal rights. In other words, the case against evangelism rests on a theological objection to any kind of absolutism and to the very notion of attempting to draw the diverse religious currents in the nation and the world into one single mainstream.

The charge of arrogance, or at least of some kind of religious absolutism, relates eventually to the claims that are made for the person of Jesus Christ. That cannot be avoided by either the proponents or opponents of evangelism. The good news that is to be propagated is quite clearly the assertion that in Jesus Christ alone we find the ultimate revelation of God, and that his life, death, and resurrection proclaim a unique victory over the forces of sin and death. There is no way for the Christian to wriggle out of the absolute claim that is being made here. Every page of the New Testament witnesses to it, and any attempts to define the gospel that are to be propagated as something other, or something less, than this are an abandonment of the historic position of the church. It has to be pointed out that these unique claims for Christ are not the invention of the church. Nor is evangelism based on the conviction that Christians have a monopoly on truth or can be proved to be wiser and better than any other people. What evangelism declares is what Jesus himself has claimed. So, far from being a matter of whether or not "our religion" is better than anyone else's, evangelism is simply a sharing of what has been found in Christ. In the words of D. T. Niles it is one starving brother telling another where to get bread. What matters is that this claim of

Christ lies at the heart of the case against evangelism as expressed by most nonbelievers and is dimly resented even by many who count themselves members of the church.

We cannot effectively evangelize in our pluralist society unless we are prepared to face this question of the uniqueness of Christ and the resistance that is bound to be met by any attempt to win others to his allegiance. This case against Christian evangelism is reinforced by the fact that no other religion, apart from an occasional and ephemeral sect, has ever made such a claim for its founder. Of the great world religions, Hinduism is the most tolerant and embracing. Instead of offering a rival lord to displace any loyalty to Christ, it encourages us to bring our Christian allegiance into the common fold where all great religious teachers are seen as aspects of the one divinity that inheres in the whole universe. Buddhism advocates the teachings of Gautama but in no way claims for him the kind of universal lordship and saviorhood that the New Testament ascribes to Jesus. Its evangelism is an invitation to embark on the Eightfold Path that leads to Nirvana, but it often expresses a desire to assimilate Christian convictions rather than to demand their surrender. Islam has proved historically to be the most aggressively evangelistic of all faiths apart from Christianity and makes no secret of its belief in the universal validity of its claim that Allah is the one true God and Muhammad is his prophet. But Muhammad is not preached as the savior who died for all mankind to bring us to God.

Judaism occupies a unique position in our understanding of evangelism. In practice it does not promote any kind of evangelizing activity. It is foreign to the Jewish tradition to attempt to win others to the religion of the law and the prophets. Modern Judaism will not reject a Gentile who wishes to become a Jew, but the invitation is seldom given, and the convert must undergo intense preparation and training. Judaism, as we learn from the violent struggles that rage in our day, means a people and a land, as well as a religion. Therefore, there is no attempt to encourage others to claim a heritage that is not traditionally theirs. Yet, strangely enough, it is from Judaism that the two most vigorously evangelizing religions have sprung—Christianity and Islam, in historical order. It is they who have made their own the prophetic pictures of a world-embracing religion where the word is, "Look unto me, and be ye saved, all the ends of the earth: for I am God, and there is none else" (Isaiah 45:20).

Thus the case against evangelism is based not only on a rejection of the claim of Christ to be *the* Way, *the* Truth, and *the* Life, but on an opposition to the entire biblical emphasis on the one true God and the apparent exclusiveness of those who claim to be his chosen. Nothing is more foreign to the climate of contemporary thought than the claim that there is one God in whom absolute truth, absolute justice, and absolute goodness are to be found, unless it be the claim that we have been found by him. This is to a high degree an age of syncretism—the reconciliation of opposing religious views and practices with the idea of arriving at a universal world religion that would incorpoate the relative truths of all the major faiths. The biblical religions of Judaism, Christianity, and Islam, when they are true to their origins, stand like a rock against this current of opinion. Christian evangelism, in particular, invites an allegiance to One of whom it is said that he is not only *the* Savior of the world but its hidden Lord to whom in the end every knee shall bow.

Arnold Toynbee, who combined historical erudition with a sensitive appreciation of the vital importance of religion in the human story, found it hard to forgive the biblical religions for their resistance to the pressures of syncretism. He was totally unsympathetic to the element of exclusiveness in the Old Testament and to the note of aggressive evangelism in the New Testament. Like many others, he demonstrated only too persuasively how the conviction that one is in possession of the unique religious truth has led to persecutions, witch-hunts, and the abomination of religious wars. He even hinted that modern totalitarianisms, such as Nazism and Communism, were offshoots of the same detestable impulse to impose one's exclusive and unique truth on every other soul on earth. He expresses as well as anyone the widespread modern conviction that in the latter half of the twentieth century, for religion, the name of the game is tolerance.

This argument is enormously appealing on every level today. The intellectual tends to take it for granted that if religion has any validity at all it must be broad enough to include the insights of hundreds of varied traditions. The notion of any exclusive claim being made for one religious personality is an anathema, and the idea of propagating such doctrine is pernicious. The same attitude is reflected by such common clichés of popular speech as, "We're all going the same road anyway," or as was said to me not long ago, "I believe in all religions."

Before we can move decisively into a new phase of Christian evangelism, we shall have to listen carefully to those criticisms and prejudices. We shall have to distinguish between the New Testament call to make known the good news and the various methods that have been used in recent years, and there will be a constant need for sensitive theological thinking in order to meet the deeply-felt objections of a pluralist society to the claim that Jesus is the Lord and Savior of the world.

II

"Beginning in Jerusalem"— The Curious History of Evangelism

A look at the case against evangelism leads to the conclusion that the word has suffered from a plethora of different meanings and associations in recent years. A great many of the objections one hears, for instance, can be met by the anwer: *"That's* not what I mean by evangelism." Even the more serious objections to the notion of persuading others to accept the Christian gospel can be fended off by what may seem to be a rather subtle distinction between evangelism and proselytism. Too much explaining of this sort may leave the impression that the word can be made to mean almost anything one chooses, from the most aggressive and intrusive kind of soul-saving to something that is more or less the equivalent of living a Christian life.

"There's glory for you!" remarked Humpty Dumpty.
"I don't know what you mean by 'glory,' " Alice said.

"I mean there's a nice knockdown argument for you," he replied.

"But glory doesn't mean a 'nice knockdown argument,' " Alice objected.

"When *I* use a word," he retorted, "it means just what I choose it to mean, neither more nor less."

To avoid, if possible, letting the word "evangelism" mean just what I choose it to mean, neither more nor less, I will dig into its history, "beginning in Jerusalem," by tracing its origin in the biblical revelation. We don't, of course, exhaust the meaning of a word merely by inquiring into its etymology. All words come to us carrying a great weight of meaning gathered over the years. If I were to call you a Pharisee, for instance, you would not be mollified by any explanation that I was using the word in its original sense to mean a scholarly layman devoted to the traditions of his religion. But to get at the meaning of a technical term like "evangelism," in its Christian sense, we have to begin by reaching back to the circumstances surrounding its first use and ask why and how it came to be employed by the primitive church—or by Jesus himself. Then we can trace its history and the activity it denotes through the centuries to the present time.

The first discovery to be made as we track down the etymology of "evangelism" is that it is a beautiful word. If it has become, as I have suggested, an ugly word for some today, this is simply because of unfortunate associations that have been attached to it. The word is, in itself, exquisite since it has the prefix *eu* meaning "good," which we find attached to happy words like euphoria, euphonious, eutopia, and eupepsia. The opposite prefix *dys*, meaning bad, giving us words like dyspepsia and dysentery. Perhaps we need the word "dysangelism" to describe some of the worst methods of spreading the Christian gospel. Then it also—perhaps you never noticed— contains the lovely word "angel." An angel is a messenger, one who brings news. So evangelism is nothing other than the bringing of good news. That rules out some false notions right away. A preacher may, for instance, feel compelled to warn certain people that they are on their way to hell, but at that point he cannot be called an evangelist; this could hardly fall into the category of good news. Nor is it good news when a preacher blasts a congregation for its indifference to social evils; he may feel constrained to do so, but this is not evangelism.

In the Bible, we find the conviction that God has good news for the confused and errant human race, and today the Word of God is first and foremost a message of joy and hope. It was a wise decision of the publishers to call one modern version of the New Testament *Today's English Version, Good News for Modern Man.* This translation is based on the assumption that people like you and me are in need of good news from God. If we happen to be of the opinion that there is nothing fundamentally wrong with us, no serious trouble afflicting the human race, no need for anxiety or distress as we look around us, or inside us, or as we contemplate the future, then we shall not be looking for good news from God or any other source. Evangelism, in any age, means nothing at all to the complacent, the self-contained, or those who believe that there is nothing the matter with the human race that cannot be cured by education, therapeutic techniques, or suitable religious exercises. Jesus remarked more than once that his news was brought to the sick, not to those who considered themselves perfectly healthy. This is why he laid such stress on the obviously needy throughout his ministry. When the disciples of John the Baptist were sent to ask Jesus if he were indeed the expected Messiah, they got the answer, "The blind receive their sight, and the lame walk, the lepers are cleansed and the deaf hear, and the dead are raised up, and the poor have the gospel preached to them" (Matthew 11:5 KJV). Notice that the climax here is not the raising of the dead but the evangelizing of the poor.

The good news of the Bible can be traced right back to Abraham. Here is the clue to the unique message of the Bible as the Word of God to mankind. If you ever wondered what good news can lie hidden in the extraordinary story of Israel with its confusing assortment of migrations, settlements, battles, laws, rituals, kings and queens, priests and prophets, as recorded in the Old Testament, you should ponder the words that Abraham heard when he set out on the great adventure into the unknown: "In thee shall all families of the earth be blessed" (Genesis 12:3). Something new was happening. Out of all the various migrations that took place in the Middle East about four thousand years ago, this one was to lead to the creation of a people who, to this day, are unique among the nations of the world. They were to be the bearers of good news from God. That is the whole point of the Old Testament story. The very thought of a chosen people disturbs our current sense of justice and has been, as we have seen, one of the chief targets of those who accuse Christians of having inherited many objectionable features from the Old Testament. But here we find the positive injunction to be evangelists—bearers of good news to the entire world. The Old Testament records with unsparing candor the continual failure of Israel to live up to this high mission—the lapse into savage nationalism, the misinterpretation of their role as chosen people to mean "God's favorites", the refusal to listen to God's call to service, the smug assurance that God is always on their side. But never is the call totally forgotten, and the prophets, while blasting the unfaithfulness of the people, kept alive the song of deliverance. Even when everything went wrong, the holy land was invaded and Jerusalem destroyed, and the chosen people found themselves exiles in a distant land, the hope never died that God was still at work through them, and that, even from their sufferings, a salvation would come, and all people would hear of the universal triumph of righteousness and peace. Such thoughts gathered around the figure of the coming Messiah, and from the depths of this people's misery

rose the triumphant shout of the evangelist with good
news for all people:

Arise, shine; for thy light is come, and the glory of the
Lord is risen upon thee. For, behold, the darkness shall cover
the earth, and gross darkness the people: but the Lord shall
arise upon thee, and his glory shall be seen upon thee. And
the Gentiles shall come to thy light, and kings to the
brightness of thy rising (Isaiah 60:1-3).

Here are the roots of evangelism in the indomitable
conviction that in spite of all human terror and
suffering God has good news for all his human
family, that he is a God who works through and with
the agonies we know to bring us the word of victory
over the power of sin and death. This is the heart of
evangelism. If we in any way claim to be Christians, it is
because this Word has come to us, and it has come
through strange channels, not through any religious
gifts of ours or our particular ancestors. If we
evangelize we must know that first we have been on the
receiving end. May this not be the meaning of the
apparently abrasive words of Jesus: "Salvation is of the
Jews?" "In thee shall *all families of the earth* be blessed."
Evangelism is rooted in the humility that recognizes
that we are in debt to those who brought this message
of universal salvation to the world. So far from its
being an arrogant presumption on our part to declare
the good news, it is a joyful debt of honor, a privilege,
and an obligation. The Word of the One God, the
Father Almighty, is addressed to everyone of his

children. Unless we are polytheists, evangelism should be an ineluctable concomitant of our faith.

We turn to the New Testament. "Salvation is of the Jews"—yes, and the one Jew in whom for us the good news breaks with overwhelming power is Jesus. In him is concentrated the entire story of his people, and in him is fulfilled the vision of a Messiah who fights the battles for us and brings the news of victory. Every book of the New Testament is written to tell us that he *is* the Good News. "These (things) are written, that ye might believe that Jesus is the Christ, the Son of God; and that believing ye might have life through his name" (John 20:31). These words from John's Gospel could be written across all the books of the New Testament. The New Testament *is* evangelism. Nobody set out to write the Gospels and Epistles as a historical exercise providing information about a remarkable teacher and the impression he made on his contemporaries. Jesus himself is not shown as an interesting talker who wanted to add his store of ideas to the common pool of religious thought and practice. He erupts into the Jewish religious scene with the reforming fervor of a prophet. But from the beginning it was impossible to fit him into the usual national and religious categories to which we assign people on the assumption that every group has its own faith and it is best not to rock the boat. He just went out and met whomever it was—Pharisee, Sadducee, Roman soldier, tax collector, foreigner, or Samaritan—and evangelized. Mark, in his hurried way, tells us that "after John was put in prison, Jesus came into

Galilee, preaching the gospel of the kingdom of God."
The Greek here says "announcing the good news," in
other words, evangelizing.

In a very short time we read of Jesus' gathering
twelve of his closest followers around him, and we are
told two things about the purpose for the founding of
this band. "He ordaind twelve that they should be with
him and that he might send them forth to preach."
Here is the embryo church of Jesus Christ, and its
function is clear: to be with him, to be closely united
with him, and to go out to tell the good news. The
evangelistic impulse of Jesus is transmitted to his
followers. This is what they have to do—to remain in
close touch with him and to go out and evangelize. It is
made clear that this evangelism is not in words only.
They were instructed to follow the Master's example
in healing, helping the poor, and giving themselves to
all in need. The good news that they barely
understood was to be demonstrated by a new kind of
living. The Kingdom that was coming with Jesus was
heralded by signs as well as words, by deeds as well as
sermons. But the central theme was unmistakable;
there was news to be told—news of hope for the
despairing, forgiveness for the sinners, life for the
dying, and victory for the defeated.

There came a time when all this evangelizing zeal
died away. Jesus was arrested and executed. The
disciples ran away. It seemed after all like a false dawn,
and these frightened men had no more good news to
tell. Then came the Resurrection. It is very soberly and
quietly told in the Gospel records, and strangely

enough it produced no immediate fervor to let the fantastic news be known. We are simply told that Jesus appeared alive to his disciples at various periods over a few days. No one else saw him, and we are given the impression of a bewildered group of men and women huddled in corners of Jerusalem not knowing what to do next. They could not forget the parting words of the Lord when he finally returned to the Father's home. He had "opened their mind to understand the scriptures" and had said:

This . . . is what is written: that the Messiah is to suffer death and to rise from the dead on the third day . . . and that in his name repentance bringing the forgiveness of sins, is to be proclaimed to all nations. Begin from Jerusalem; it is you who are the witnesses to it all. And mark this: I am sending upon you my Father's promised gift; so stay here in this city until you are armed with the power from above. (Luke 24:46 NEB).

And armed they were. Luke tells us that some days later the Spirit came with power on the group of disciples, and the whole picture changed. From being a confused group of Jewish believers trying to understand how they were meant to continue their identity as followers of Jesus, they became dynamic evangelists joyfully and courageously announcing the good news to anyone who would listen. And their good news now focused on Jesus Christ, crucified and risen, the Jesus in whom God had met and had conquered the powers of darkness. Evangelism, in the full Christian sense of the word, had its beginning at Pentecost.

It began in Jerusalem. This is the link with the good
news given to Abraham, the good news that was
celebrated in the song of the psalmist and the music of
the Temple. For the first few months Christian
evangelism was Jews telling Jews that they had found
the Christ. Then the book of Acts tells how the Spirit
broke down the barriers and sent the disciples of Jesus
out into the gentile world. First, Peter, then Paul, was
dazzled by the revelation that the news of the victory of
Jesus Christ was to be conveyed to every nation of the
inhabited world. (The Greek for "inhabited world"
was *oecumene*—that is why we can speak of the
ecumenical mission of the Christian church.) What we
are watching is the spread of the gospel south to Egypt
and Africa, and north to Syria, Asia Minor, and then
into Europe. The strategy seems to have been to make
for the big cities and fan out from there. Their tactic
was to approach the synagogue first, which often had a
number of gentile adherents, and then to use every
opportunity to speak in whatever forum was offered.
There was no fixed formula for the message, but it
always centered on the person of Jesus as the Lord and
Savior and the decisive victory he had won over sin
and death.

This was a time, not unlike ours, when millions were
adrift from the ancient religions, when there was
widespread fear and anxiety, when many sought the
mystic path and were attracted by the mystery
religions of the East. Gibbon summarized the religious
situation with his usual insight and somewhat cynical
wit when he wrote: "The various modes of worship,

which prevailed in the Roman world, were all considered by the people as equally true; by the philosopher, as equally false; and by the magistrate, as equally useful."

At this period there was no question of a Christian holding back from the task of evangelism on the grounds that we should leave each section of the human race to enjoy its own religions. It was, like ours, a highly volatile situation where people moved readily from one set of beliefs to another. Where the Christian message was not penetrating, other messages were—as they are today. The Christian church set itself the conscious task of out-living, out-loving, and out-thinking every other creed or philosophy in the field with a vigor and enthusiasm that is matched today only in those areas where the Gospel is a relatively new arrival on the scene. For the first three hundred years or so, it was the passion for evangelism that accounted for the spectacular growth and expansion of the church, an expansion not again to be matched until the nineteenth century. The notion of a settled church, that felt no obligation to pass on the news, had not yet emerged.

A turning point in the history of the church—one which was to lead to some radical changes in its concept and strategy of evangelism—came with the conversion of the Emperor Contantine and his establishment of Christianity as the official religion of the Roman Empire. The legend is that before his decisive victory over a rival for the imperial title at the Milvian Bridge in 312 A.D. he saw the sign of the cross in the sky with the inscription, In This Sign Conquer. Soon after he issued an edict giving religious freedom to all sects, and then he later declared the Christian faith to be the official religion. The nature of his conversion has always been a matter of debate since, arguing that baptism was the sacrament that immediately granted absolution of all one's sins, he postponed his own baptism until his deathbed.

For some this moment in the history of the church represents the spectacular triumph of the gospel, the greatest success story in the records of evangelism. For others this is the great betrayal, the beginning of the transformation of Christianity from a dedicated minority into a complacent majority; from a dynamic prophetic movement that worked like leaven in society, injecting the good news of the gospel into a hostile world and challenging the assumptions and pretentions of the ruling power, into a popular religion that entered into an unholy alliance with the state. Triumph or disaster: arguments for and against validity of Constantine's conversion and the subsequent total change in the worldly status of the church will go on until the Lord's return. What concerns us here is the effect of this event on the concept and practice of evangelism.

No one really knows what the leaders of the church at this time conceived their obligation to be in the matter of spreading the good news and winning converts under the new conditions. Obviously the tide was running in the church's direction. Once Christianity had shaken off its image as a small, obstinate, and persecuted sect, and had become the recognized religion acceptable to the governing powers, the average man or woman took little persuading to enter the fold of the church. Here is the origin of the dilemma that has haunted evangelism up to the present time. Should the church welcome the support and encouragement of the civil authorities, or should it not? On the one hand, the risk of both official and popular support for the gospel is that the demands of Christian discipleship will be watered down; that the differences between the ethics of Jesus and the ways of the world will be blurred; that the word "Christian" will come to mean little more than decent, acceptable, respectable, and that in the end the state will simply swallow up the church into some kind of department of religion. On the other hand, we find that this process has often meant the Christianizing of the powers that be and the penetration of the good news into every level of society. It is the church, it is claimed, that converted the state to such humane concerns as education, care of the sick, and respect for human life. Again, today there is an inner contradiction in the fact that even evangelists who lay most stress on a radical conversion that separates the Christian from the world are notoriously eager to elicit the support of presti- gious figures from presidents to baseball stars.

For several hundred years after Constantine, the church was adjusting to a new position in the world. Within a certain territory where Christianity was dominant, the pressure to evangelize seemed to be off. Gradually, it came to be accepted that to be born was to be baptized and drawn into the enveloping nurture of the church. Evangelism would then consist in little more than the "Christianizing" of each successive generation. By the Middle Ages, this was the dominant concept, and the power, riches, and prestige of the institutional church were such that the notion of there being any unbelievers to win to Christ in the community was almost unthinkable. Any such were not regarded as targets for evangelism but rascals to be rooted out of the body politic. This is when *miscreant*—which literally means believing wrongly—came to have its current coloration.

Evangelism in the sense of extending the church into regions where the gospel had not penetrated had continued into the late Roman Empire and throughout its decline. Some of this was conducted by saints who were within the New Testament tradition of passionately wanting to let the whole world know of the good news of salvation. But the church was rapidly being corrupted by its power and resources, and evangelistic movements often took the form of a power-play by which whole tribes were forced, more or less, into the faith. By a method that has been rudely described as "hosepipe baptism," masses of pagans were swept into the embrace of the Christian church. These are some of the more perplexing episodes in the curious history of evangelism. The fantastic aberration known as the "Crusades" also dates from this period. With all its aura of romance, heroism, and extraordinary dedication, a crusade could be described, in part, as evangelism at the point of the sword. This may seem absurdly irrelevant to our situation today, but from all such misadventures we might learn the lesson that a gospel of love cannot be promoted by force—whether that be military, economic, or (our temptation today) psychological.

At the time of the Reformation and even subsequently, there was surprisingly little change in the attitude of the churches toward evangelism. Purging the church of much notorious malpratice and recovering the power of the word of God did not lead immediately to a passion to win converts either at home or abroad. The rule still was that a state had an established religion, Catholic or Protestant, and in each case the church devoted iself to the nurture of all citizens in the faith and the Christianizing of each successive generation. There were sects such as the Anabaptists who attempted to live and witness like first-century Christians and evangelized with the fervor of many fringe sects today. But they were regularly condemned by the official churches as fanatics, enthusiasts, or worse. Catholics, Lutherans, Calvinists, and Anglicans concentrated on the upbuilding of Christian society, and though there were efforts to reclaim the lapsed and bestir the indifferent, little thought seems to have been given to evangelizing the part of the world the gospel had never reached.

What we have been discussing is the concept of Christendom—the idea of a community of faith coterminous with the nation—or with Europe as a whole. (I have had to neglect the other great sections of the church, notably the Orthodox, which lost contact with the West and developed an even stronger alliance with the state. Evangelism for the Orthodox would be understood in terms of drawing all into the liturgical life of the church.) In the sixteenth century, the French essayist Montaigne expressed the popular view when he wrote: "We are Christians by the same title as we are natives of Perigord or Germany." The concept of Christendom dies hard, especially in those countries that still have some kind of an established church. Even in the United States with its separation of church and state, it is not uncommon to hear expressions like "This is a Christian community" or "the Christian West" and to sense the assumption that Christianity is somehow permanently woven into the fabric of our common life.

It was in the eighteenth century that sensitive Christians began to wake up to the fact that Christendom, in the sense of a great bloc where the faith was taken for granted and the church was in permanent alliance with the state, had broken up and that strange new currents of thought were abroad, many of which were either hostile or indifferent to the Christian cause. It was a revolutionary age in which century-old habits of thought and action were disappearing, and masses of human beings were becoming almost totally detached from the church. Thus evangelism began to grip the minds of alert and concerned individuals and groups of Christians in almost every section of the church. This was the age when so called "foreign mission" began to appear. The command to go into all the world was again taken seriously, and the heroic epoch of missionary adventure began. In spite of the abuse that has been hurled at this movement, either as a species of religious colonialism in which the Bible followed the gunboat or as a wrong-headed attempt to foist a European style of life on the happy native, we should recognize not only the sincerity of the motives that animated the missionary pioneers but their extraordinary influence in counteracting the worst effects of the colonial period. The history of Africa and the liberation struggle, which we are now witnessing in all its complexities, would have been totally different were it not for this missionary effort.

During the nineteenth century, the church was gradually recognizing that vast numbers in so-called Christian countries were drifting away from the faith and becoming sensitive to the call to minister to the victims of modern forms of human exploitation and oppression. This period also saw the proliferation of evangelistic movements of all kinds in Europe and America, and these often combined the appeal for commitment to Christ with practical efforts to alleviate all kinds of human distress. These included campaigns for reform of unjust laws and the introduction of new legislation governing such matters as slavery and child labor. Throughout the nineteenth century there were awakenings of evangelical nature in many countries, and it is useful to reflect that many of these were actually opposed by established churches. John Wesley was a loyal member of the Church of England

and remained so until his death, but the resistance to what they called enthusiasm on the part of church authorities forced him to take a more and more independent path. Similarly the conventional churches were often strongly opposed to movements like the Salvation Army, the campaigns of Moody and Sankey, and the revivals that became a feature of American life. Sometimes the criticisms were directed to the crudity of the theology or the extravagance of the emotions aroused, but there was also a kind of hangover from the days of Christendom. It was vaguely felt that there was something indecent in addressing any respectable citizen as if he were a lost sinner and that there was something unseemly in the thought of anyone getting saved in a Presbyterian or Episcopalian church.

The twentieth century has seen another gradual change in the attitude of the church towards evangelism. First, the devastating effect of the upheavals of world wars and economic depressions coupled with the emergence of the *ersatz* religions of Communism, Nazism, and various brands of nationalism has shattered any remnants of the idea that such an entity as Christendom any longer exists. Great areas of the world where the church was once firmly established have pased under communist control. Christian worship, Christian ethics, and Christian influence on public life has ceased to play strong national roles in almost every country of the West, even in the United States where church membership has been extraordinarily, and perhaps deceptively, high. So the traditional churches of every hue have been driven to reconsider the question of evangelism. Soon after World War II, a book appeared in France entitled *La France—Pays de Mission?* which typifies the kind of thinking that came to dominate the latter half of this century. Every country is seen once more as mission territory, and evangelism is recognized to be desperately needed everywhere—and not just among the down-and-out at home and the heathen abroad.

There has also been a lively theological movement that has explored again the gospel as recorded in Scriptures. The biblical meanings of sin, salvation, redemption, liberation, and life eternal have been re-explored, freed from the clichés into which they often had been locked. The very agonies of this century—modern warfare, the threat of the bomb, concentration camps, the return of torture, the dehumanizing process—demand the rediscovery of the good news of the victory of Christ and its urgent proclamation to every human being on this planet. We are far from the relative securities of the nineteenth century, far from the rationalist religion of the eighteenth century with its confidence in the Supreme Being, still farther from the medieval picture of Christendom, but now, perhaps, not so far from the apocalyptic atmosphere in which the New Testament was written. I find myself more at home in the atmosphere of the Gospels or Paul's Epistles than I do in that of some familiar hymns that date back seventy years. We are in a world where the eschatological rings a bell that was not heard when many of these hymns were written. "Where sin abounded, grace did much more abound," wrote Paul. It is when sin seems to come to a climax, sending tremors and convulsions through the human race, that the church is summoned to shout aloud the good news of God's redeeming grace.

Who needs it? Everybody needs it. Evangelism today begins in the hearts and minds of those who call themselves Christians. Through them it spreads to the neighbor who is living in fear and often in despair. It is no longer an optional activity for any Christian or any church. It was not an option when begnning in Jerusalem the disciples fanned out to give the news to the entire known world, and it is not now. "I had most need of blessing," cried Macbeth with blood on his hands, "and 'amen' stuck in my throat." Isn't that a picture of our bleeding world, and can the "amen" of God's blessing stick in the throat of his church? "In you, shall all the families of the earth be blessed." It was his promise to Abraham and his descendants and to the New Israel which is the Christian church.

III

The Way, The Truth, The Life— in a Pluralist Age?

Some years ago I was driving back from the funeral service of a very remarkable old lady, one of a generation that found joy in the worship of the church, generously supported its missionary efforts, and combined a tolerant and liberal outlook with an untroubled conviction that Christ is indeed the Lord and Savior of the whole world. In our conversations we had roamed over many topics, and I was always stimulated by her lively mind and rich experience of life and braced by the radiance of her faith. She had traveled extensively, but I do not recall our ever having a discussion about the claims of Christianity to be unique among the religions of the world or of the legitimacy of the ideas of mission and evangelism. In her world such activities were quietly accepted as obligations of discipleship—without fuss or debate and without any trace of intolerance or arrogance.

In the car as we returned to New York from the distant cemetery, I found myself talking to another generation—her grandchildren. After some polite words of appreciation about the service, one of them said he wanted to raise a question about a passage of scripture that I had read. "It's that bit from the Gospel," he said, "where Jesus says he is the way, the truth, and the life; and what really bothers me is the statement 'no man cometh unto the Father but by me.' I find that intolerant." Since I have read from the fourteenth chapter of John at every funeral service I have ever conducted, I was a little surprised to be challenged about its theological implications—surprised but delighted for here was someone who had really listened and had not just been lulled by the beauty of the words. It was refreshing to realize the impact of the claims of Christ on one of a generation not disposed to accept uncritically the assertions of the Christian church. If I had tape-recorded that conversation, which lasted us until we reached the city, I should have much of the material for this chapter, for my questioner was, of course, raising the key query of the theology of evangelism—the claim of Christ to be *the* way, *the* truth, and *the* life. He was more conscious than his grandmother ever could have been of the fact that Christianity today exists as one option among many in the religious field and has to justify, modify, or abandon its claim to be unique. Since that conversation I have been more and more conscious of the need to clarify this question, and hope I would not be totally satisfied with the answers I used then. The rapidly changing religious scene in this country and across the world makes this challenge to the evangelist more acute.

This is why, with some hesitation, I added to the claim of Christ in the title of this chapter the words: "in a pluralist age." For years I have resisted using "pluralist" since it is an example of imprecise jargon we could well do without. I find that a comparatively modern dictionary still defines pluralism in its historical usage as meaning: (1) the philosophical theory that there is more than one basic substance or principle, thus contrasting with dualism or monism; or (2) the ecclesiastical situation where one person holds more than one office at the same time. Since I doubt whether one in ten today who uses the word is at all interested in this philosphical debate or in the niceties of ecclesiastical politics, I had to track down a dictionary recent enough to have caught up with the way in which the meaning of this word has changed over the years. Here is what most people today seem to have in mind when they talk about pluralism: a condition of society in which numerous distinct ethnic, religious, or cultural groups coexist within one nation. Once I had that, I became even less sure that I should use this slippery word, for there is nothing particularly new or revolutionary about a state of affairs where numerous distinct, ethnic, religious, or cultural groups coexist within one nation. Only when a government attempts to exact conformity to one particular church or ideology can pluralism be said *not* to exist.

It should be said right away that the Christian church and Christian evangelism should be perfectly content with such a pluralist society. This is one aspect of our question that can be disposed of fairly simply today. There have been times when the church was *not* prepared to coexist with other religions or with unbelievers. Both Roman Catholic and Protestant churches have attempted in the past to impose their faith on whole populations arguing that those who resisted were in error and therefore had no rights. It was to escape such imposition of a common religion that the early settlers in this country set out on their great adventure, but unfortunately it has to be recorded that soon after some of them were busily establishing their own brand of the faith with an equal intolerance and persecuting zeal. For centuries now Protestant denominations have given up all ambition to exercise a religious monopoly or even, with few exceptions, to claim a privileged position for their church. The suspicion, however, lived on that the Roman Catholic Church would always seek a privileged position from which to dominate the religious scene and would inevitaby seek the power to weaken, if not persecute, those outside its fold. The Declaration on Religious Freedom of the Second Vatican Council should have disposed of such fears. Today no body of Christians in its right mind would dream of seeking to impose its faith on others by statute or coercion. A gospel of the love of God is by its very nature unenforceable, and those who propagate it should have no worries about living in a society where numerous distinct ethnic, religious, and cultural groups coexist.

Christian evangelism has, in fact, thrived under the Constitution in the U.S. where according to the First Amendment, Congress shall make no law respecting an establishment of religion. But it is also worth noting the words which follow, "or prohibiting the free exercise thereof." Pluralism is sometimes interpreted in such a way as to suggest that the amendment is designed to prevent the propagation of any particular religion or at least to encourage the view that religions should stay put within their own borders and make no effort to evangelize. But evangelism, as we have seen, is integral to the Christian faith. We are charged to make the good news known. Therefore to forbid evangelism would most certainly be prohibiting the free exercise of the Christian religion. That this is not a merely academic point is shown by the legal situation in Communist countries where freedom of religion is limited to public worship and evangelism is specifically forbidden and only atheism has the right to be propagated. This is not to say that evangelism becomes impossible under such circumstances—it has been illegal many times in many countries—but the Christian church has an interest in claiming for the gospel the same freedom that should be granted to other religions or ideologies. Milton expressed the Christian ideal when he wrote: "Give me the liberty to know, to utter, and to argue freely according to conscience, above all liberties." And he touched on the soul of evangelism with these words: "Though all the winds of doctrine were let loose to play upon the earth, so Truth be in the field, we do injuriously by licensing and prohibiting, to misdoubt her strength. Let her and Falsehood grapple; who ever knew Truth put to the worse, in a free an open encounter?"

Since the charge of intolerance is frequently hurled at the church when the good news is proclaimed as an invitation extended to the entire human race with the clear implication that Jesus Christ is unique and incomparable, it is important to recognize that such an attitude is perfectly compatible with the acceptance of the rights of other faiths to hold and to propagate their own convictions. It is not only compatible, it is implicit in the nature of the gospel which not only respects but exalts the freedom of the human will. It is an offer of love, and love by nature cannot be enforced. There is nothing in the least inconsistent about a Christian welcoming this kind of pluralist society where everyone may choose how, or whether, to worship God; and holding in the greatest respect venerable religious traditions quite different from his own; *and* at the same time announce his belief that Jesus Christ is *the* Lord and Savior of the world. The greatest theologians, missionaries, and evangelists I have known, either personally or by their writings, have been men and women of the broadest sympathies and utmost respect for the freedom of the human spirit in all the varieties of its religious affiliations. No one in recent years has more rigorously contended for the uniqueness of the gospel and been more adamant in proclaiming Christ as *the* way, *the* truth, and *the* life than Karl Barth; yet those who knew him could testify to the breadth of his understanding, the warmth of his humanity, and the catholicity of his friendships. You can be convinced that Jesus Christ is the sole Savior and Lord without becoming a fanatic who condemns all other faiths and despises the aspirations of the humanist and agnostic.

So Christianity welcomes this so-called pluralist society. Yet, there are reasons why evangelism today has to reckon with it as never before. This country, for instance, may have been officially pluralist from its foundation; but for many years there was a latent assumption that Christian doctrines and Christian ethics were the accepted norm, and it would still be difficult for, say, a candidate for political office to win election on a platform that specifically repudiated conventional religious convictions. There is, however, a very noticeable change in the religious climate, a change that has been even more marked in the countries of western Europe. The winds of secularism have been blowing hard, and the conception of a pluralist society now is one in which there are virtually no unifying spiritual or moral convictions, and Christanity takes its place as one of a number of tolerated religious traditions which are regarded as having little influence on the destiny of the modern world. The younger generation is, therefore, encouraged to assume that religious conviction is a more or less private matter with little or no relevance to the powers that are determining our human future. They may adopt one or another of the old or new religions, and the impression is given that it doesn't really matter which, since none are of world-shaking consequence. In such circumstances it would seem mildly ludicrous to assert that the central figure of the Christian religion is the unique Lord in whom the entire world can find salvation and that the good news he embodies is the message that all men and women need to hear.

The new pluralism also has meant that we are all far more conscious of the presence in our world of faiths quite different from traditional Christianity. Fifty years ago a student could pass through high school, and college, and settle into a job without once being confronted seriously by adherents of religions other than Christianity. How ever great the perennial interest of the young in comparative religion, there used to be little chance of other faiths being encountered as live options. The situation now is very different. I am not thinking only of those areas where the Jewish presence is articulate and impressive, but of the great increase in travel whereby students are constantly in contact with representatives of other religions; of the phenomenal spread of cults like Zen Buddhism, Hare-Krishna, and other imports from the East; and of the new vitality of Muslim teachings in various forms.

The effect of this is either to promote a rejection of the Christian absolutism of the past and the adoption of a rival faith, or to encourage the search for a new world religion that will incorporate what is seen to be most valuable in the various traditions. The latter course, known as syncretism, has a very great appeal to those who are most conscious of the secularist trend that threatens the existence of any religion at all. Faced with the enormous power of an atheist materialist ideology most evident in the communist countries, but penetrating everywhere, those who value the spiritual aspect of human life know it is imperative to close ranks and not let any inter-religious squabbles weaken a common front. In such an atmosphere pluralism would seem to demand that Christianity drop its unacceptable claims for the uniqueness of Christ.

Before we examine again the claim of Christian evangelism in this pluralistic world, we ought to stop to question some modern secularist assumptions.

First of all, the belief that Christian convictions have no validity beyond the individual and his private satisfactions and that they, with all other manifestations of religion, can be shunted aside as of no serious account in a world dominated by secularist thinking and technological skills, needs to be challenged. History (which may be returning as a mentor after the antics of the "now" generation) reveals that it is ideas, and particularly religious ideas, that have shaped the course of every civilization the world has known. And, like it or not, the most powerful ideas have been those associated not with broad religious generalities, but with quite specific doctrines and one dominant personality. Moses, Buddha, Jesus, Muhammad—names that have affected the lives of millions and decisively determined the course of human events. The Western civilization which we have inherited was the product of many strands of thought and energy—Hebrew religion, Greek philosophy and art, Roman order—but without the influence of the Christian church with its constant evangelism, there would be no such thing. You might even say that the entire fabric of law, literature, art, music, philosophy, government, social service, science, and medicine came into being because there were those who unquestioningly believed that Jesus Christ is the way, the truth, and the life.

It has been assumed that the period of such religious influence on the totality of life is long past and that modern society has no need of any unifying world view such as was provided for centuries by the Christian gospel. The great themes of creation, fall, and redemption are often considered as merely interesting myths that sustained another period of human art and morals. Yet, as was noted by Walter Lippman in the twenties, no rival world view has emerged to give direction and stability to the human enterprise. For a time it seemed as though a common cultural inheritance would form the basis of the new secular Western civilization, but it has proved quite inadequate to sustain any common ethic or accepted meaning for the human drama. Without vital religious belief centering on such a world view as is offered in the Bible, our civilization is floundering in a morass of subjectivism in which life more and more approximates the theater of the absurd. If a pluralist society is one in which various religions and cultures coexist, but none is regarded as having anything true to say, any contact with reality, then the Christian should be one who is ready to say with Paul: "I am not ashamed of the gospel of Christ: for it is the power of God unto salvation." Our world is starving for people who have found something worth believing and are prepared to declare and commend the gospel that speaks of *the* way to a lost generation, *the* truth to those who have been brainwashed into believing there is no such thing, and *the* life to those whose prevailing philosophy is one of despair and death.

We need to look more closely at the assumption that our new awareness of the presence and vitality of faiths other than Christianity must lead us to modify the claims of Christ. It is true that an increased knowledge of other religions must have the effect of delivering Christians from narrow-minded prejudices and the insufferable air of superiority reflected in hymns which dismissed great civilizations and venerable religious traditions with such words as: "The heathen in his blindness / Bows down to wood and stone." If pluralism means that Christians are now in a better position to understand and appreciate the insights and practices of other religions, then it should be welcomed by all who are concerned with the propagation of the gospel, for the cause of Christ is never served by ignorance and contempt for rival faiths. But if pluralism is taken to mean that we now are compelled to acknowledge that all religions are equally true, equally valid, and simply alternative ways to the one God, some protest is in order.

We are so bemused by the dogma of relativism today

that many actively resent any suggestion that a particular belief either about God or man is true and that, therefore, a quite different view must be false. This amounts to "dogma of relativism" for that is what it is. I am reminded of the following conversation between a Christian lecturer and a student who maintained that there was no such thing as any absolute truth:

"Are you sure there are no absolutes?"

"Yes."

"Are you *absolutely* sure?" Silence.

I have the greatest respect for the devout Buddhist who believes that what is known as Nirvana in his religion represents the truth about the ultimate destiny of the human pilgrim. I happen to be convinced that the Christian doctrine of eternal life is true. But no juggling with words and ideas could make both true. Similarly, there are many common beliefs between Christians and Moslems about the nature of God, but there are points at which a clear choice must be made. "God is love." Is that true or is it not true? A very liberal Jew and a very unorthodox Christian could agree that their religions were almost identical, but an orthodox Christian and an orthodox Jew both recognize that, with all the common bonds that exist, a real matter of truth is at stake: Was Jesus, or was he not, the Messiah or Son of God?

The attraction of syncretism, the attempt to construct a world religion based on the common belief in the reality of the Divine, lies in its relativist suppositions. There is indeed a pressing need for the great religions of the world to enter into fresh dialogue, to cooperate in confronting a materialist philosophy and in humanitarian efforts. But a synthetic world religion that ignored the clear differences of conviction would be an anaemic and powerless body. For it would bypass the question of truth and be productive of people without conviction. It is comparatively easy to bring together vaguely affiliated Jews, Christians, Muslims, and Buddhists on the basis of some lowest common denominator of belief; but such an amorphous body would have little impact on the secular world. Effective and vital religion always has in it the note of particularity. And a particular personality, a particular doctrine, always raises the question of truth or falsehood.

If we transfer the idea of pluralism to the scene of world politics, I think most of us would agree, for instance, that we would prefer to live in a world where communism and Western democracy coexist rather than blow each other to pieces. But surely that does not mean that we see no essential difference between them, or that we can talk happily about their being different roads to the same end. Here again is a question of truth. We have to take a stand. And, as Solzhenitsyn keeps reminding us, if we are so bemused by the vision of détente that we forget this choice and abandon our convictions, we are in deep trouble. The relativism that evades decision has infected us in every aspect of modern life and is the cause of the loss of nerve that Solzhenitsyn deplores.

The Christian, in the New Testament sense of the

word, is one who places his confidence in One whose claim is: "I am the way, the truth, and the life." The supremacy of Christ as the revealer of God and the Savior of men is not a dogma dreamed up by an aggressive and intolerant church. It is simply the response to his claim. You cannot read the New Testament in such a way as to eliminate the news that in Jesus is both the unique revealer of God and, by his death and resurrection, the bearer of a unique message of liberation for the whole human race. In the last hundred years there have been repeated efforts to edit out of the Gospels any such claims and references, but these efforts are now generally admitted to have failed. Whether you believe them or not, this is what the eyewitnesses to this momentous event had to say about Jesus and his mission on earth. They recorded him as the revealer of God making such stupendous claims as "He who has seen me has seen the Father," and of his universal saviorhood: "The Son of Man has come to seek and to save that which was lost, and to give his life a ransom for many," "I, if I be lifted up, will draw all men unto myself"; and the three astounding words: "Come unto me." Those disciples were not philosophers arguing a case. They had nothing at all to say about how these claims were to be reconciled with the existence of other religions. As two of them told the authorities in Jerusalem after Pentecost when they had been told to stop talking and teaching in the name of Jesus, "We cannot but speak the things which we have seen and heard." That is the continuing motive of Christian evangelism—the compulsion upon those who have met the Risen Christ to pass on the news.

In this age of pluralism there is, of course, something offensive to many in this claim of Christ to be the way, the truth, and the life. So be it. There is always the risk of offense when we take a stand on anything we believe to be true. I am not now attempting to soften the challenge of the Christian gospel so as to make it appear a reasonable version of the common convictions of the religious minded. From the beginning, the gospel was hard to take—"unto the Jews a stumbling block, and unto the Greeks foolishness." The type of Christian apologetics that has recently taken the line that nearly everyone is really a Christian at heart and that sprinkles the water of baptism on every fad of the modern mind seems to me both contrary to the New Testament and vaguely insulting to the believer. (If I were an agnostic I wouldn't want to be patted on the back and assured that I was really a Christian.) The business of the evangelist, and every believer is called to be one, is to present Jesus Christ in humility and sincerity as what he claimed to be—the revealer of God and Savior of the world.

The way: According to John's Gospel, Jesus spoke these words in reply to a question from Thomas. Jesus had been speaking about his return to the presence of the Father and had told the disciples that they knew both where he was going and the way to follow him. Thomas, expressing the confusion and doubts that assail everyone who wants to know how to reach through to God himself, protested: "We don't know where you are going, and how can we know the way?" "I am the way," said Jesus. The key to our understanding of this claim lies in the mysterious name Son of God. This metaphor is the clearest we can have to illustrate what we have come to call the Incarnation. As Son of God, Jesus reveals in human terms who God is: "He who has seen me has seen the Father." It is not as if we already knew all about God and then had to wonder how Jesus could possibly be related to him in this way. Our knowledge of Jesus *is* our knowledge of his Father. This is how we are to understand the words that troubled my young friend so much: "No one cometh unto the Father but by me." The accent is on Father. He doesn't say, "No one can have any knowledge of God at all unless they have heard of me and listened to me." We forget that this belief in the Father God is a legacy of the gospel, not something that was universally held. And we should remember that no other great religion makes this claim for its founder—that he not only taught about God but revealed him in his very person. You can examine the teachings about God offered by religious leaders including Jesus, and make comparisons. But you cannot, even in this pluralistic age, compare this claim of Jesus to be the Son of the Father, and the way to him with any other; for, apart from the deranged or the occasional messianic figure, no such claim is made.

Christianity, before it was so called, was often known simply as the Way. That meant not only that the Christian evangelist offered news of Jesus as the way to a living relationship with the Father, but that he himself had not yet arrived. This is important to keep in mind when evangelism begins to sound smug and self-satisfied. Yes, this is the way, but how much traveling we still have to do, and how much we have to learn from other travelers with totally different backgrounds from ours! The tragedy has been that evangelists have sometimes defined the way in terms, not just of Jesus and all he still has to show us, but of their own rigid code of behavior or their own stereotyped plan of salvation.

The truth: Again we are reminded that the gospel we are commending claims to be true—that is, to correspond to that which is *real* and not illusory. Our pluralist age, as we have seen, is remarkably indifferent to the question of truth. That is why a great variety of religious doctrines can be accepted as equally valid. And the modern church has fallen in with this habit of mind by commending the gospel on almost every possible ground—except that of its truth. We proclaim that it works—that following Jesus produces certain very desirable results like peace of mind and inner strength. We assert that the gospel solves our problems. "Jesus is the answer," we read on bumper stickers, while our cynical contemporaries add "But what is the question?" We hint that Christian discipleship will raise the morale of the nation, rescue the young from decadence and the old from despair, and form a bulwark against communism. Some, or all, of these things might indeed follow from a widespread response to the Christian gospel, but I find that the promises of Jesus to would-be disciples are much less attractive (losing one's life, taking up a cross, suffering, persecution); and that his appeal is to the truth that he brings us all—truth about ourselves, truth about God, truth about salvation, truth about the way ahead. Jesus said, "I am the truth."

Again we have to keep in mind that the truth is in him and not in any particular body of his disciples. He had a horror of any group of people who exalted their own religious traditions into a fixed and final truth. His own truth cut into the most sacred texts to bring new light and meaning—"You have heard it said . . . , but I say unto you." Conversely, his claim to truth was a challenge to those relativists in the pluralist world of Rome. In a famous scene he declared to Pontius Pilate: "To this end was I born, and for this cause came I into the world, that I should bear witness unto the truth. Everyone that is of the truth heareth my words." And —Pilate said, "What is truth?" And, as Bacon remarked, he "did not stay for an answer." It is Jesus who again confronts a cynical world with his word of truth, and evangelism is nothing more than letting him speak. There must be no claim that our church, our tradition, our theology has a monopoly on religious truth. The evangelist has no need to deny the truth that lies in other faiths, and indeed may see them as the reflection of that light which, as the prologue to John's Gospel tells us, is "the true light which lighteth every man that cometh into the world."

The life: In our pluralist age this sounds like the arrogant assertion that the Christian life is the only life worth living. There is indeed a form of evangelism that suggests that God is inviting everyone to conform to a style of life similar to that of those who deliver the message. And, looking at some of them, a natural reaction is, God forbid! I believe this word of Jesus goes deeper than the question of our style of life—which, in any case, can vary enormously within the Christian fold. I wonder how we have given the impression that Jesus wanted a homogeneous band of disciples. Conversion to him should make you more real, more individual, than you were before. *Life* is a key word in the gospel. It stands for the unique Christian announcement of the bringing of life out of death, the story of the Son of God going through death and hell for us to bring us his resurrection victory. This is a different story from any other being told in this pluralist age. It is the liberating news that God himself has rescued us from the powers of sin and death. No other religion tells of a real savior who fought the battle with the powers of evil by allowing himself to be done to death before being brought back triumphantly to life. It is a story of something that really happened, once and for all, on this planet. It cannot be undone, and it cannot be repeated. Yet, when we receive the Lord of life, we share in the victory. This is the incomparable Jesus the church is bound to proclaim.

Let me now attempt to summarize the kind of

answer I would give to any who resent the announcement of the universality of Jesus and the uniqueness of his gospel: "I agree that this is a stupendous claim that we are making, and I should in many ways be happier if I could suggest that Christ is only one way among many to a knowledge of the Father-God, represents one truth that needs to be supplemented by others, and offers to give life in much the same way as leaders of other religions. But I can't. For this is not my choice, but his; not my claim, but his. Once I have met with him and known something of what he is and what he has done for me and all the human family, I cannot set him on the throne of my heart as one Lord among many, I cannot say to him: 'Thanks for your truth, but now I'll go elsewhere for more.' I cannot conceive of a better way, a richer truth, a more abundant life to be found in some future Savior. So I am glad to be able to say with conviction, but I hope with no presumption, the answer to the first question of the Heidelberg catechism: ('What is your only comfort, in life and in death?') 'That I belong—body and soul, in life and in death—not to myself but to my faithful Savior, Jesus Christ.' In so doing I pass no judgment on others who, for one reason or another, cannot make this answer. The Christ I believe in is the Light who shines wherever human beings have turned to God in worship and in prayer. I believe, with the apostle Peter, that 'God has no favorites, but that in every nation the man who is godfearing and does what is right is acceptable to him.' But I also believe that all who have, in any way, been captivated and liberated by the way, the truth, and the life of Jesus, are bound to pass on the news. And I expect that, beyond the narrow confines of my own Christian traditions, I will be led by others, in the great human family, to discover more of what it means that Jesus Christ is Lord."

IV

How and Whom Do We Evangelize Today?

It would be reasonable to ask at this point just who the "we" is in the title of this chapter. The simplest answer is that "we" refers to all who, in general, accept the point of view about evangelism set forth in the previous chapters. So a short summary of what has been said is in order.

In the first place, we realize that evangelism has unfortunate associations in the minds of many of our contemporaries. We are very much aware that the methods employed by certain evangelists of the past hundred years are open to question on rational, psychological, and even moral grounds. The image of Elmer Gantry still hangs around, and many are quick to suspect any mass-evangelism movement of hysteria, manipulation, and fraud. We are also conscious of the popular resistance to the message of evangelism, especially when it is presented as an intrusion in the private convictions of one's neighbor or as an arrogant assertion of the superiority of our religious beliefs. We are, that is to say, alerted to the fact that if we are to practice evangelism today, we cannot ignore the built-in prejudice against it, not all of which is to be written off as totally unjustified.

In our world we are not in the position of the early Christians who went out into a society that knew nothing whatever about the gospel and had never experienced the impact of various styles of evangelism. Nor are we like those missionaries who in more recent times were announcing the good news to people untouched by the Christian church. Evangelism today has to be done by those who are sensitive to the fact that the modern world has been saturated by Christian ideas whether recognized or not and is disposed to reject any attempt to sharpen them in such a way as to present a clear-cut call to decision. We must be people who understand the modern revulsion against anything that looks like intolerance or absolutist claims in the field of religion, are prepared to think hard about the distinction between proselytism and evangelism, and are prepared to repudiate unworthy methods of presenting the good news or exerting pressure for its acceptance.

In the second place, we are people who are not prepared to let popular prejudice or the relativism that rejects the claim of Christ to be the truth, or even the worst excesses of personal or mass evangelism, silence the clear call of Jesus to "go forth and make all nations my disciples." We are convinced that the good news has to be told and that from the beginning the church was a movement of evangelism. We see ourselves as part of the fruit of the worldwide mission of the Christian church and not as the possessors of a white Anglo-Saxon religion that we are trying to impose on others. We see no way whatever of divorcing our Christian faith from the obligation to share it, or of eliminating from the New Testament the note of evangelism. We discard the myth that the world or the nation is neatly divided into static religious groups that ought not to be disturbed, and we are alive to the tremendous changes that are sweeping across the globe, as rival faiths and ideologies compete for the allegiance of the human soul. We are persuaded then that Christianity is, in its very nature, an outgoing religion, that the good news is meant to be continuously promulgated, and that the church is not a museum in which a certain religious tradition is preserved, but a mission with a message for everyone within reach.

In the third place, we have come to terms with the stupendous claim of Jesus to be the way, the truth, and the life. Our own decisive encounter with him leaves us no alternative. In a pluralist society we recognize the freedom of a great variety of religions, as well as atheism, to exist and propagate their beliefs but are impelled to declare *our* belief that Jesus Christ is the Savior of the world. We humbly, but firmly, believe that he is the unique revelation of the Father-God, and that by his cross and resurrection, good news of salvation has dawned upon the world. We do not attempt to decide just how God relates this salvation to the various sections of the human family or to individuals: We are not judges but heralds who make known the news that "God was in Christ reconciling the world unto himself." We do not think of ourselves as having discovered all there is to know about Christ, but we do know that we have been grasped by him and have found him to be the universal Lord. As Paul put it: "It is not to be thought that I have already achieved all this. I have not yet reached perfection, but I press on, hoping to take hold of that for which Christ once took hold of me." The Christ who once took hold of us is not one whom we can enshrine with other lords in the temple of our souls or think of as one way to God among many or as bearing a truth that may well be superseded or imparting a life that is not available for all.

With such an attitude and with such convictions, how do we go about the business of evangelism in this last quarter of the twentieth century, and who are the people to whom we should be declaring the good news? In the long story of the church, evangelism has taken many forms; and although the target has been scripturally defined as "all the world," specific groups of people have often been singled out as being in special need of the gospel, as the most likely to make a response, or as having a strategic importance for the growth of the church. There is little use in being intellectually convinced that evangelism is a legitimate and necessary activity for the church in every age if we are not prepared to think hard about how we can best practice it in our generation and who the people are we want to reach with the good news of Christ. Jesus once spoke sharply to his disciples about interpreting the signs of the time, and the Christian church has made its greatest advances under the guidance of those who were alert to the spirit of the age and the contemporary currents of history. We might protest that the spirit of our age is one of the greatest confusions and that the currents of history are running so swiftly we cannot keep pace, but there is in this very confusion and accelerating change an urgent call to find new ways to present the gospel and discover where our energies should be directed.

Behind all our thinking and planning, however, there must be a confidence that God is still at work in his world. It is presumptuous on our part to think of evangelism as depending entirely on our skills and energies. The good news, after all, is a declaration of what God has done, is doing, and will do for his human family through Jesus Christ his Son. It is not a party line developed by the church that we are trying to propagate or some psychological gimmick we have to offer to straighten people out. The New Testament makes it clear that it is the Holy Spirit, and not the evangelist, who does the "converting" and that Christ is already present in the very places where we try to present the gospel.

Some years ago a legend about Jesus was circulating briskly among those who wanted to stimulate Christians to more active evangelism. The risen Lord has returned to heaven and the archangel Gabriel has the following conversation with him:

Gabriel: What plans have you made to continue your work on earth:

Jesus: I have chosen twelve ordinary men to be my disciples.

Gabriel: And if they should fail?

Jesus: I have no other plans.

The first time I heard this I was mightily impressed. So Jesus relies on us, his disciples, and the whole enterprise depends on our faithfulness! Then the old Calvinist spoke within me, and I began to question this implication that God is impotent, unable to save his human family unless you and I are on the job. It is indeed a miracle that Christ commits to people like us the task of passing on the good news in word and deed, but we must have the humility to believe that he is at work whether we are in action or not and that indeed we are called to do no more than reveal to others that they are already his.

D. T. Niles has some startling things to say about this.

We call people non-Christians, and forget the full implication of the fact that for them too Jesus Christ has already died. The foundation of our preaching is the universality of the gospel. . . . We do not take the gospel to someone to whom Jesus does not already belong. . . . It is important to remember this truth in all our evangelistic work because it will save us from treating those who have not yet confessed Jesus as their personal Savior as people who are outside Jesus. In our evangelistic work we are not seeking to make people become what they are not already. We are simply seeking to tell them what and who they are. The prodigal in the far country is a son away from home. He is no one else, he is nothing less.

These remarkable words come from one who was, in a very modern sense, a world evangelist and who was throughout his ministry constantly in contact with Hindus, Muslims, and Buddhists.

This is what gives theological backbone to our evangelistic enterprise and delivers us from the daunting proposition that we are expected to devise methods to win over an alien world to the Christian religion that we profess. We have often forgotten how the first evangelists went about their work with a song of triumph in their hearts. They believed that Christ had really redeemed the entire world, that Jesus had seen "Satan as lightning fall from heaven," and that in heaven the song was already being sung: "The kingdoms of this world are become the kingdoms of our Lord, and of his Christ; and he shall reign for ever and ever" (Rev. 11:15). Niles tells us that in the meetings of the evangelism department of the World Council of Churches that great French Protestant Pierre Maury would often suddenly exclaim: "This is a saved world."

Peter, Paul, and the other apostles evangelized in the certainty that God had indeed "visited and redeemed his people" and were not long in discovering that "his people" meant the entire human family.

And they discovered that wherever they went, whether it was Peter finding himself in a Roman officers' mess, or Paul talking to the Athenians in the Areopagus, God was there already. They never acted as men hawking a new religion, which they had to sell to an alien people around the Roman Empire. They were delivering the news of the Cross and Resurrection to men and women for whom Christ had died and in whom they were to be made alive.

This understanding breaks down the element of hostility that can mar Christian evangelism, the grim feeling that somehow we have to break into enemy territory. Sure, the enemy is there, but it is human beings whom God loves that we are approaching with the news of liberation and of life. Effective evangelism is never done by the timid or the angry, but only by those who deeply love and are prepared to say to anyone at all: "God loves you. Christ has redeemed you."

How then do we find the people today who need to hear this from us, and how do we make this gospel known? It is, of course, easy to say that a Christian by his or her mere presence, attitude, and way of life, is a witness to the gospel among all kinds of people. A church on the corner is similarly a witness to the gospel for all who see it. But, from the beginning the Christian gospel would not have gone very far through the mere presence of Christians and the places where they worshiped. The gospel had to be articulated and ways found whereby all manner of people could be led to understand what the message was. But it does remain true that a Christian person and a Christian community (not just a building) are by their very existence agents of evangelism, and never more so than today.

We shall return to this theme. Meanwhile I want to select several areas of modern life where we are being specially called to evangelize and try to think through what our approach might be and how we can best invite a positive response to the good news.

Growing up around us is another generation. There was a time when it was assumed that Christian parents communicated the faith to their children, had them baptized, instructed, and confirmed in membership of the church. Generation after generation were then, as it were, automatically evangelized. There were, of course, evangelically minded parents who were not satisfied with this apparently natural acceptance of and growth into the faith, and who looked for some kind of conversion experience by which their children could be evangelized; and there were instances where a son or daughter would deliberately reject the faith in which they were raised. (*Father and Son,* the classic autobiography of Edmund Grosse, is a devastating account of such a revolt.) In general, however, the covenant theology that lay behind the practice of infant baptism produced successive generations of Christians who did not seem a natural target for evangelistic effort.

No one needs to have it explained that, over large sections of the population today, this picture has almost vanished. To a surprising degree the natural religious links between the generations have been snapped. One can find all sorts of reasons for this without indulging in tiresome nonsense about the generation gap. For one thing the younger generation today is growing up in a society that is rapidly abandoning the traditional ties with the Christian faith. And, since home life has been disrupted by modern styles of life and invaded by television, children are exposed to a secularized and unbelieving world as never before in this country's history. Then the influence of public schools where religion of any kind is taboo and where the King James Bible is the one classic that is forbidden (and also of private schools most of which have been scrambling for years to divest themselves of any trace of their religious ancestry) leads to a climate of thought that is anything but hospitable to the Christian faith. It must also be admitted that a recent generation was not altogether wrongheaded in rejecting what seemed to them a merely conventional and morally empty churchiness on the part of their elders. An even more recent generation is searching again for the mystical and the transcendant but, with some exceptions, is not finding a satisfaction in the Christianity of the established churches.

So here is a great field for evangelism, and it should not be left to those who offer the most dogmatic presentation of the gospel, the most rigid interpretation of the Christian life, and the most emotional kinds of religious experience. This does not mean that the established churches should wage a polemic against mass youth movements that exhibit these traits or that they should criticize the youngsters who claim that through these movements they have found new life in Christ. I keep remembering the remark of D. L. Moody to the clergy of his day who found fault with his methods of evangelism. "I like my way of doing it," he said, "better than your way of not doing it." It is for us to awaken to the vital importance of youth evangelism within the community life of our churches and to accept the responsibility of teaching, demonstrating, and commending the gospel of Christ to the coming generations whose exposure to and understanding of religion may be wholly different from our own.

Hence, there is an urgent need for reinforcements in the field of what we know as Christian education. Congregations have been apt to think of Sunday school, Bible and confirmation classes, and youth clubs as traditional activities to be taken care of by a few specialists and enthusiasts. In fact, this kind of Christian education is not much more than a hundred years old, and in this country at least it shows alarming symptoms of decline. Most churches find it exceedingly difficult to recruit volunteer teachers and often fail to recognize the enormous importance of their work as the evangelizers of the next generation. There is a tendency to consider the clubs and organizations for children and teen-agers as convenient channels for "keeping them out of mischief" rather than as vital communities where they may discover the power of the gospel in word and action and fellowship. Beyond the church walls there is a vast potential for evangelism in a generation that seems to me to be extraordinarily frank and open about their beliefs and disbeliefs, and ready to respond to an equally frank and open presentation of the gospel. My impression is that they respect a clear and genuine conviction even when they are unable or unready to echo it but see through any attempt to inveigle them into conventional church life by gimmicks and diversions. And in their search for real community, they know the difference between the group that is a pale imitation of what they can find elsewhere and a group that is held together by the depth of friendship known in the New Testament as koinonia.

Another segment of society that has been notoriously neglected by Christian evangelism is that of the intellectual. Not for a minute would I suggest that there is an elite whose education and interests mark them off from the rest of the human race and who therefore must be approached with deference and awe. When I was a university chaplain and had to listen to many sermons by visiting preachers, I was wearied by those who felt it necessary to display their academic credentials by delivering sermons in which the sound of the gospel, if it were there at all, was smothered in the intellectual jargon of the schools. If a speaker consulted me about the assignment I used to say: "For God's sake remember that professors and students are ordinary sinners like anyone else." Yet it is plain that, by and large, in recent years the church has not succeeded in winning for Christ the intellectual leaders. Atheism and agnosticism are almost standard for the average faculty member. The Christian gospel is seldom discussed as a live option among the philosophies of life. Look at any review of books today; how often does either the author or the reivewer show any trace of Christian conviction? This is reflected again in the bookstores. I was in one recently where I hunted in vain through all the sections for one marked Religion, eventually finding in a corner a few shelves marked Mysticism and the Occult. In a nation where over half the population are avowed members of a Christian church and probably less than 5 percent are concerned with the occult, this seemed a strange state of affairs. The answer must be that church members are not considered people who read books and that books written by churchmen will have no appeal to the average intellectual.

If this is true then we have failed to evangelize a very influential segment of the population. The cult of simplicity, the desire for easy reading on the part of the average Christian, the suspicion of the theologian as the one who complicates the obvious, and the refusal to take seriously the commandment to love God "with all your mind" has led to a dangerously false division between faith and thought for many Christians. On the one hand are the devout who believe the gospel, read the Bible, say their prayers, attend worship, and attempt to put their faith into practice. On the other hand are the intellectuals of the church who are sealed in their seminaries and colleges idulging in all kind of wild speculations and occasionally announcing to a bewildered public some startling discovery as, for instance, that God is dead. This, of course, is an exaggerated picture, but what the French call *le trahison des clercs* ("the treason of the intellectuals") is a very real description of the attitude of the devout to those who engage in an academic study of religion. They are regarded with suspicion while anyone who can write a popular book with sparkling real-life illustrations to bolster the faith is regarded as doing all that ought to be done to interpret the gospel for the literate.

No other generation has been so threatened by this dichotomy. From the earliest days the Christian church challenged the intellectual world with the story of the crucified and risen Christ, and within a few centuries their gospel began to dominate the thinking of the West. While there were always Christian intellectuals who deviated from the orthodox creeds, no one imagined that to apply one's mind with the utmost vigor to the content of the Scriptures inevitably led to abandonment of the faith. From the liveliest arguments with the so-called heretics there emerged the towering intellectual figures of the Fathers of the church; then later, Aquinas, Calvin, Erasmus, and the great succession of thinkers who have left an indelible mark on the history of human thought. To this day there are within the church—and faithful to the content of its creeds—men and women whose intellectual stature is equal to that of the secularist or humanist in any field. What has been lacking is the skilled and effective middleman to interpret the theologians' apprehension of the gospel to the educated public, to expound the faith with intellectual integrity but without the technical language of the schools. The enormous impact of C. S. Lewis, who combined a genuine piety and loyalty to the biblical faith with a literary flair and sparkling wit, is the measure of our desperate need for just this kind of interpretation of the gospel. How much encouragement have we given to young men and women with literary gifts and intellectual power to give themselves to this ministry?

But such work of apologetics is only one aspect of evangelizing the intellectual. The world of art and culture has been notoriously empty of Christian witness in our time. Protestantism, in particular, has had a somewhat unfortunate artistic history to overcome and is having a hard time in overcoming the tradition that the story of Jesus is best conveyed in shoddy art and third-rate music. We need a generation of convinced Christians who will express their faith, not in words of intrusive evangelism, but in novels, poems, plays, pictures, and music that are informed by the vision that the gospel gives them. It would be safe to say that more are converted to Christianity today through the symbol, the image, the communicated vision than through the arguments of the most skillful apologist.

This leads me to a brief comment on what could be called the "evangelism of the institution." By institution I mean the spheres of influence in modern society—the arts, the media, law, politics, unions, science, medicine, welfare—the powers of which we are very conscious. Can such institutions be evangelized? The answer is no, if by evangelized we mean the total Christianizing of these forces, their capture by the gospel of Christ. Yet the church has contantly made the attempt and during the Middle Ages succeeded, at least nominally, in bringing every institution under the control of the gospel. In our time promoters of the so-called social gospel have sometimes been imbued with a similar ambition, and the vision of the kingdom of God on earth led to dreams of the total Christianizing of the state and all its institutions. The bitter experience of the rough element of human sin that is even stronger in the institution than in the individual and does not yield to any mass conversion, and the insights of such thinkers as Reinhold Niebuhr, Karl Barth, and more recently Jacques Ellul, have taught us not to look for any such spectacular Christianizing. Nor does the New Testament give us any encouragement to expect it.

Yet, the church would be unfaithful if we failed to recognize the opportunity to penetrate every institution with the word of the gospel. Too often Christians have simply abandoned them to the secular powers, and the individual Christian whose work takes him into politics, law, or journalism, for example, feels that his or her sphere of witness is limited to personal behavior and style of life. Yet, there is obviously a tremendous work of pre-evangelism to be done. By pre-evangelism I mean the influencing of opinion, the changing of the climate of opinion, the softening up of secularist assumptions, the raising of Christian ethical considerations—all those things that help to create an atmosphere in which evangelism becomes more possible and effective. What we call the media is a case in point. The enormous impact of what is read, heard, and seen today hardly needs underlining—especially in time of presidential election. It is often said that the journalistic ideal is one of complete objectivity and neutrality, but it is increasingly recognized that there is really no such thing. It is impossible to distribute news without some principle of selection. It is impossible to highlight issues without some philosophy to indicate what the real issues are. It is impossible to discuss controversial matters without revealing what one's bias is. What is often described as objectivity in ethics or religion is in fact a hidden philosophy of rationalism and secularism. Here is a field for pre-evangelism. We need skilled and convinced Christians who will see to it that the Christian view does not go by default and who will be awake to the conditioning of the public by rival philosophies.

If we turn our thoughts to one of the traditional targets of evangelism—the lands where Christ is not known—what are we to say in the light of modern conditions? In our day we have seen the demise of the term foreign missions. The phrase goes back to a time when Christians in the Western world awoke to the fact that great areas of the world had never been evangelized and rightly felt that since they themselves were the product of a foreign mission, in the distant past, they were under an obligation to obey literally the Lord's command to "go into all the world." The period from 1810 to 1910 saw a fantastic spread of the church right across the world, and events today in Africa and Asia have been to a great extent influenced by this extraordinary wave of evangelism. The question is now: Is such an objective still part of the Christian obligation to evangelize? And, if so, how?

The foreign mission did not, of course, stop dead in its tracks in 1910. But that was not only a year that marked the end of an era just before the convulsions of 1914 and the fearsome era it heralded; it was also the year when Christian missions were gathered in a world conference at Edinburgh, and a new concept of missionary strategy was born. This was the dawn of what we call the ecumenical movement, which has dominated the thinking of most world strategists of the gospel ever since. From then on the term "foreign mission" was doomed.

That concept of evangelism assumed the existence of a Christian home base from which expeditions were made into foreign territory with the news of Christ. Now we have become aware that there are no such firm Christian home bases any longer. We also realize that the gospel is anything but a Western possession that must be exported, warts and all. Today we use the term "world mission" because ecumenism has taught us to think, not of Christian countries sending missionaries to foreign parts, but of one global church that is engaged with the non-Christian world on a front that runs through every country in the world. Within that world mission, it is true the more established churches with greater resources may still be called upon for considerable contributions of people and funds, but the traffic is no longer one way.

What this means is that we have not lost the vision of "going into all the world" but have abandoned the thought of going it alone. World evangelism today means the drawing together of Christians in all countries, learning from and supporting one another, in order that the gospel may be proclaimed in word and action at each point of tension with the forces of unbelief, and to the uttermost parts of the earth. We believe that it is *his* world.

From the far horizons let me turn in conclusion to the next door neighbor. What are our responsibilities as Christians for the people we know best, our friends, our colleagues at work, our literal neighbors? The very thought of evangelism in this area may send shivers down our backs. It suggests the very kind of embarrassment and intrusion that disrupts friendships and severs natural relationships. We still are inclined to accept the cultural ban imposed by all hostesses of a previous age on the discussion of politics or religion at the dinner table and dislike what has been referred to as chatting Christ over the coffee cups. And there is a peculiar resistance to sharing religious experience with those who are very close to us.

Yet, may we not be allowing some limited notion of what evangelism is to distract us from the genuine desire to share what we believe to be immensely valuable with our nearest neighbors? Isn't there something wrong if we profess to believe that the good news is for everybody but have no concern about passing it on to those we see every day? I remember a meeting of students in Edinburgh that took place after a mission conducted by D. T. Niles. He had asked all Christian students to gather in order to make plans for following up the mission. Right away he asked a question: "How many of you have friends who are atheists or agnostics?" Almost everyone raised a hand. Then he asked, "Do you ever feel sad about it?" All of us, I think, were a little stunned by the question for we realized that, far from feeling sad, most of us were secretly rather proud of the number of non-Christians we counted among our friends. But wasn't Niles speaking right to the point? For one who knows the joy of believing and the presence and power of Christ, there should be a sadness that this is missing from the lives of those we are fond of. But what can we do about it?

For one thing we can be less reticent than our fears dictate when the subject of religion does come up. Today the old barriers about the discussion of religion have come down, and a surprising number of people are ready to talk about their beliefs or disbeliefs. In the same way when other controversial topics arise there is often a quite natural opportunity to indicate that your point of view is influenced by your Christian belief. Still more important is a readiness of Christians to be alongside friends in times of distress or anxiety—not with a string of texts or assorted pieties, but with genuine Christian concern. If someone is in our prayers, what could be more natural than following up with the kind of care that is itself a strong witness to the gospel we believe?

In the same way, a congregation that is active in the world mission of the church, ought not to be oblivious to the needs of the people in its neighborhood who have no living faith in God or any real knowledge of the gospel. How easily we settle into the ruts of an institution that provides worship and pastoral care for its members and Christian education for its children, shares in many valuable activities, plays its part in the wider mission of the chuch, but does little about bringing the gospel to those who live next door.

This is perhaps our most difficult task, and there are no easy answers. But there is one thing we *can* do: We can insure that the *koinonia,* the deep fellowship of a church, never becomes a closed shop but remains ready to enfold any lonely stranger who comes our way. One of the answers to how to evangelize is right here. In our day a person who may not respond to a declaration of the grace of our Lord Jesus Christ or even to a demonstration of the love of God, may first be drawn toward the gospel by a real experience of the fellowship of the Holy Spirit.

What this kind of evangelism implies is a local church that is a truly living community of faith. This means not only a congregation that is nourished and inspired by biblical preaching and teaching, but one that is really learning to worship in Spirit and in truth—with both a communal sense of the divine and with sincerity. A church that offers merely a vague experience of togetherness, or an assortment of comforting religious clichés cannot be an instrument of evangelism in an age that seeks both the supernatural dimension and a natural, genuine humanity.

I believe that the searching agnostic or the confused would-be believer responds to worship that is both natural and supernatural and is instantly repelled by all that is *unnatural.* Hence it is vitally important for the pastor, the organist, the worship committee, and all who have special responsibility for public worship, to be constantly alert to the evangelizing potential of weekly worship and to keep asking the question, "Is what we offer on Sunday the very best we can do to glorify God and enable a stray visitor to glimpse what that means?" This note of reality should, of course, also be struck on occasions like funerals and marriages. These are times when we are in contact with many who are outside the normal church family and who are susceptible to the power of the gospel as expressed in a sincere and carefully prepared act of worship. Needless to say, baptisms also afford a unique opportunity for challenging young parents with the question of what it means to confess Christ as Lord and Savior and to raise their children in that belief.

Churches today are, of course, only too anxious to try any methods or movements that promise to add new members to their rolls. It would be hypocritical of me to pretend that I am uninterested in the statistics of my church membership, but I need constantly to remind myself of the true motive of evangelism—the making and nourishing of Christians. An alert leadership will, therefore, evaluate all invitations to join in campaigns and crusades in this light, realizing that in the end it is not some extraneous personality or organization that will lead to successful evangelism but the congregation itself. I believe that all our churches can benefit from the ecumenical experience of sharing in an evangelistic campaign whenever it can be done with integrity and enthusiasm.

My own experience leads me to conclude that some of the most effective evangelism being done in the churches today happens where small groups are formed within a congregation, meeting probably in members' homes. The focus of the group may be the study of a book, experience of prayer and meditation, or simply a free discussion of the content and meaning of Christian faith. Such groups can be based on age, on common interests, on literary or artistic concerns—or they can be formed from a cross-section that mirrors the entire congregation. It is within such groups that men and women of all ages and temperaments are finding their way into the adventure of discipleship.

The only excuse for not having an evangelism committee in a local church is that every committee, from administration to worship, gives evangelism priority in its agenda. Such a state of affairs would reflect the neglected truth that evangelism is happening in every legitimate activity of a Christian church. The gospel reaches our contemporaries in dozens of ways beyond the evangelistic sermon. Music, drama, poetry, current affairs, social action—when these and many other activities of a lively church are dedicated to the glory of God and in Christian love, the evangelical power is beyond our calculation. Perhaps Protestants, in particular in our recent flirtation with the arts, need to understand that these are neither propaganda nor entertainment but avenues to be pursued with integrity to the glory of God and in celebration of the gospel.

Finally, if evangelism is communication, we must be more alert than we have been to the revolution through which we are living. We need a Christian strategy for this electronic age. To paraphrase Paul, "How shall they hear without Christians who know how to use the media?"

V

The Crux: Have You Anything to Declare?

Those of us who enjoy visiting other countries are familiar with that solemn moment when at the frontier we encounter a customs official who has one look at our assorted possessions spread out on a table, fixes us with steely eyes, and asks, "Have you anything to declare?" I have not yet had the nerve to answer, "Yes; as a minister of the gospel, it is my duty to declare that Jesus Christ is your Lord and Savior." Instead I experience that slight feeling of guilt that comes over the most honest of us at such times. Have we forgotten something? Should we have mentioned that tie or pair of socks? Even if our consciences are perfectly clear, we are quite sure that we *look* guilty.

As we have been examining together the true nature of evangelism, recognizing how integral it has been to the life of the church from the beginning, hearing again the unmistakable claim of Christ to be the Savior of the world, realizing how many areas of evangelism demand our urgent attention right now, have you felt an even greater sense of guilt? I have. It is impossible to be exposed to the New Testament evidence, to the example of the greatest saints of the church and some Christians whom I know, and above all to the words of the Lord himself, without admitting that I am a "slothful servant," a poor communicator of the very gospel that means so much to me. Our real problem is not so much being convinced that evangelism, properly understood, is clearly our duty and should be our joy, it is responding to two little words that hang on the curtain in my study in memory of the first favorite sentence of my little boy, "Do it."

The truth is that most of us are reluctant evangelists. What I am after in this chapter is the real cause of our reluctance.

We can begin by comforting ouselves that there is good biblical precedence for reluctance in offering ourselves for such a task. When Moses had his vision of God at the burning bush in the desert and heard the surprising command, "Come now therefore, and I will send thee unto Pharaoh, that thou mayest bring forth my people the children of Israel out of Egypt," his immediate response was: "Who am I, that I should go unto Pharaoh, and that I should bring forth the children of Israel out of Egypt?" (Exodus 3:10-11). And when Gideon was busy about his daily chore of threshing the wheat and the angel of the Lord appeared and said, "The Lord is with thee, thou mighty man of valor" (Judges 6:12), he replied, in effect, "Who? Me?" And when the young Jeremiah was told, "I ordained thee a prophet unto the nations," he showed no enthusiasm for the assignment. "Then said I, Ah, Lord God! behold, I cannot speak: for I am a child" (Jeremiah 1:5-6). Even the disciples of Jesus huddled together in Jerusalem after the Resurrection and showed no enthusiasm for telling anyone about it until the fire of the Spirit descended at Pentecost.

What we have in common with these people in the Bible is a sense of inadequacy. We are persuaded, as they were, that we have no natural gifts for being in any sense communicators of the gospel, let alone effective evangelists. We satisfy ourselves that this is proper humility. "Who am I that I should attempt to evangelize my neighbors, let alone the world?" Church members today are very sensitive to the charge of hypocrisy. For years they have been caricatured—usually by people who know next to nothing about any church at all—as men and women who cloak their natural vices by an assumption of spiritual superiority and claim to be better than their pagan neighbors. In forty years of ministry I have met very few church members who were afflicted with this kind of pharisaism and even fewer who claimed to be better than their neighbors. But I have met dozens of people unconnected with any church who have both implied and openly stated that they consider themselves morally superior to most church members they have known. It seems to me that the Pharisee of Jesus' parable is more usually represented today by the person who says: "I thank God that I am not as other men are, extortioners, unjust, adulterers, or even as this church member." While it is the church member who is saying, "God be merciful to me a sinner."

What the Bible tells us is that a genuine humility of this kind is the basis for service in God's name. If Moses, Gideon, Jeremiah, or the disciples had been people whose attitude was, "Here I am, Lord—just the very person you need," they would have sunk without trace in the quicksands of history. Evangelism, as we have seen, is primarily God's business, and what he needs from us is our ignorance to be enlightened, our impotence to be empowered, our emptiness to be filled. The one disqualification for his service is the conviction that we are just the people he most needs. We may accuse Paul of hyperbole, even of a mock humility, when he speaks of himself as the chief of sinners, but every line he wrote indicates that he lived in constant amazement that God had chosen him to be an evangelist for Christ. He was not a man given to underestimating his natural gifts, deferring to the opinions of others, or playing down his status as an aristocratic Jew and a man of Greek culture and Roman citizenship. But when it came to his calling as a Christian evangelist, what he said was: "Unto me, who am less than the least of all saints, is this grace given, that I should preach among the Gentiles the unsearchable riches of Christ" (Ephesians 3:8).

As an excuse for our reluctance to do anything about evangelism, this plea of sinfulness will not do. There is not a single case in the New Testament of a man or woman being chosen to make Christ known because of their outstanding virtue and sanctity. The twelve disciples were not in any sense what the East knows as holy men. And among the characters we find disseminating the good news are people like the woman with a lurid past Jesus had met at the well who, without waiting until she had become a different person, went right back to tell her neighbors about the Lord ("And many of the Samaritans of that city believed on him for the saying of the woman" (John 4:39); the ignorant and despised character who had only one answer to make to all who challenged his loyalty to Jesus, "Once I was blind: now I can see"; the wretched Zacchaeus who, within minutes of meeting Jesus, was announcing to all and sundry the revolution he had created in his life; the Roman officer who was inspired by a vision to throw a party so that Peter might tell his friends about Jesus; or even the brigand hanging on the cross whose last words have rung through the years as a witness to the Savior, "Lord, remember me when thou comest into thy kingdom." If it is "just a I am" that I receive the grace of the Lord Jesus Christ, and the love of God, and the communion of the Holy Spirit, it is "just as I am" that I am called to make this salvation known. There is no standard model of the Christian evangelist, no stereotype of piety and zeal. The same Christ who receives us with the words "Come unto me" is the one who says, "Go into all the world and make disciples." The same Christ who supplies all our needs empowers us to be his evangelists.

If lack of sanctity is no excuse, neither is ignorance. Many Christians today confess to feeling tongue-tied when attempting to pass on the good news because they are not equipped to answer the questions that may arise. They are afraid that they do not know their Bible well enough; that they cannot really explain just how Jesus can be Lord and Savior of a modern man or woman; that they may well be stumped by such questions as: "If the coming of Jesus was so decisive why do we have so much misery still in the world?" or "What are you Christians really doing about the misery and oppression and injustice that afflict millions today?" or "How does your God of love let these starving babies die?" All sensitive Christians must feel a terrible inadequacy at times when confronted with the powerful arguments of the unbelieving world? Why then can we say that ignorance is no excuse? It might look like a very valid excuse for not exposing ourselves to embarrassment or even ridicule.

The first thing to say here is that we are and always will be ignorant. There are some questions to which any honest evangelist, no matter how well instructed, must answer, "I don't know." The slogan "Christ is the answer" ought not to be flaunted as if his followers had solved all the problems that have baffled the philosophers, the statesmen, and the scientists. There is an ignorance that can be freely confessed while we give our witness to what Christ means to us. It is simply expressed in the words of this hymn:

> I know not how that Bethlehem's babe
> Could in the Godhead be;

I only know the manger child
  Has brought God's life to me.

I know not how that Calvary's cross
  A world from sin could free;
I only know its matchless love
  Has brought God's love to me.

I know not how that Joseph's tomb
  Could solve death's mystery;
I only know a living Christ,
  Our immortality.

Yet, after all, we share this ignorance with every human being, believer, and unbeliever. No religion, no ideology, no philosophy exists that offers a totally rational explanation of the mystery of human life. If evil is a problem for the Christian, so is goodness for the atheist. No intellectual answer has ever been found to the paradox of free will and predestination. No movement has ever escaped the judgment that its theories are betrayed by its practice. All we can say is that the Christian story, once accepted, offers at least as rational an understanding of this mysterious universe as any other that has been proposed.

The second thing to say is: Although we should take more seriously than many do the obligation of the Christian disciple to respond not only to the invitation "Come unto me," but to the immediately following invitation "Learn of me," and for this purpose give more time to becoming instructed in the faith; we are not required to be theologians before we are evangelists. It surprises me to note how Jesus sent out his first disciples on a mission before they could have had much time to study what the message was or how they were to go about the healing task. We are just told that "when he had called unto him his twelve disciples he gave them power." It was a spiritual power by which they were to attack the evils that afflicted their neighbors, and they were to preach the kingdom of God." "These twelve Jesus sent forth," we read, and they had to make do with such instruction as they had managed to acquire. The main point was the power that Jesus gave them. So it was after Pentecost that the apostles launched the most effective and world-embracing religious movement that has ever been known. We are told that they had this power, but the religious authorities "perceived that they were un-learned and ignorant men." If they had waited for the learning and had taken their ignorance to school for a year or two, the Christian mission might never have been launched, and you and I might never have heard of Jesus Christ.

This reluctance to accept the task of evangelism until we are spiritually and mentally equipped, has not only stifled the witness of individual Christians in our time, but it has caused a paralysis that has smitten the churches. Any lively congregation today is concerned about such things as its impact on the neighborhood in the name of Christ, its failure to enlist a significant proportion of the younger generation in his cause, its inability to transcend social and racial barriers with the message of the gospel, its limited share in the total mission of the universal church. There is a sense in which great numbers of our contemporaries in their isolated apartments, in the slums, in the universities, in the arts, in industry, and in politics are looking at us and asking: "Have you anything to declare?" And we seem to be answering: "Wait a moment; we've got to put our own houses in order; we've got to discover what we really believe; we've got to do a self-study; we've got to set up committees on evangelism; we've got to analyze the social and religious situation; we've got to study the complexities of the modern mind. Then we'll be with you." The devil must be delighted by the success of his favorite strategy in the United States: Get them to analyze evangelism, to discuss its techniques, to make it a problem, to elaborate on the machinery; then they won't evangelize.

Evangelism, like every other activity of the church today, needs to be humanized. There must always be some kind of planning going on, some agencies for developing strategies and organizing campaigns of various kinds, some specialists in the theology and practice of evangelism; but the heart of it is the sharing of the good news among real people. Something has gone wrong when we begin to think of the evangelist as a religious technologist, the presentation of the gospel as a matter of mass indoctrination through expert techniques, and consider the people to be reached as church fodder, statistics to be added to our rolls. The Bible is the great corrective for this kind of thinking. It speaks from time to time of strategies, of movements, of councils, of deliberations, and of crowds; but its emphasis is always on human beings in all their rich diversity and in the warmth of personal relations.

One example from the Old Testament is the picture of King David waiting at the city gate for news of a decisive battle. When the messenger arrives what is his question? Not "Give me a report on the outcome" or "Show me the casualty statistics"; but "Is the young man Absalom safe?" Then in the New Testament, the campaigns of Jesus and his apostles are never described in impersonal terms. When Jesus was faced with the question of his relationship to what looked to many like a parallel or rival mission headed by John the Baptist, we do not find him saying to his disciples: "Draw up a contingency plan for penetrating John's movement with the gospel," but simply "Go and tell John what things ye have seen and heard." Then there are these names that keep cropping up in the Epistles. Paul, in his epistle to the Roman church, after ranging the universe in the most masterly exposition of the gospel ever penned, ends up with affectionate greetings from those who were with him: "Gaius mine host, . . . Erastus the chamberlain of the city saluteth you, and Quartus a brother" (Romans 16:23). The gospel is about people. There is little use talking of master-strategies of evangelism if we are going to forget Gaius, Erastus, and Quartus.

Evangelism takes place where you and I are in contact with real people *as* real people. This is where the witness of the ordinary church member is of vital importance. We know surely by now that the very people who most need to hear the good news—the rootless, the secularized, the cynical, the confused, the oppressed—are the most unlikely to flock to evangelistic meetings and would seldom think of entering a church. The gospel will have to come to them through their friends or acquaintances whose lives are transparently centered on their faith in Christ. This by no means implies that we have to adopt the mask of the official church member and plead for the agnostic friend to become one of us. We simply share the faith as human beings who have some basic common needs. The Chinese philosopher, Lin Yutang, who returned to the faith in his later years and became a member of the church I serve in New York, happily realized that to confess his faith in Christ did not involve assuming the mask of the conventional churchman, but he remained to the end of his days the brilliant individualist he always was, while unafraid to confess his Christian discipleship. What we need most of all today to propagate the gospel is a growing number of non-professional, truly human, unpretentious disciples whose loyalty to Christ is unmistakable and who will be the carriers of the gospel by just being their true selves. What we do *not* need is a body of pious proselytizers who seek to mass-produce Christians in their own image.

But this raises questions. How am I to become such a loyal and convinced disciple—an infectious carrier of the Christian gospel? and the corollary, How can the churches as we know them breed such people?

When I declared that we should be getting on with the job instead of waiting until all the studies were in and we felt equipped to be evangelists, I was not for a moment suggesting that we have no need to be evangelized ourselves. Along with the thrust out into the world, there must always be a returning to the source of our own faith and hope. The blunt fact is that if our churches are not conspicuously winning others to the cause of Christ today, the real reason is an inner lack of conviction about the truth of the gospel and the supremacy of Christ. By and large, in the Western world, the churches of the major denominations have tended to settle for a soft religion that peddles what Dietrich Bonhoeffer called cheap grace. We are easily content with a genial churchmanship that makes a few demands and tends to baptize everything within sight in the name of sweetness and light. Or else we strive to make up for a lack of inner commitment by a flurry of activity in good causes or by pronouncements on the controversies of the day. The remedy is not to revert to a grim and dogmatic posture that repels the sensitive inquirer or to close down our social activities and retreat from the world into a bastion of piety. It is to make sure that we are putting first things first. And the first thing for any Christian, for any church, is loyalty and obedience to Jesus Christ our Lord. It must be in his spirit, and with his power that we welcome all kinds of people into the fold of his church and that we address ourselves to the burning questions of our splintered world.

"Come unto me," said Jesus. He says it to us. Who needs evangelism? We do. The churches do. Does anyone suppose that the names that can be read by the millions on the card indexes of church membership today represent men and women who have all yielded themselves, body and soul, to Jesus Christ as their sole Savior and Lord? We rightly refuse to set rigid rules for church membership, but the lack of loyalty and enthusiasm is there for all to see. Somehow in our churches it is possible for a man or woman to drift along without ever being challenged with the good news that demands a decision. The gospel becomes a vague set of beliefs that never springs to life. The sacraments that speak so powerfully of the new life in Christ have been tamed so that they become routine observances of our ancestral religion.

It has often been remarked to me that we preachers have a habit of talking as if everyone in the pews was a convinced and active Christian—with the possible exception of Easter Sunday when we side-swipe the once-a-year worshipers. We could more often keep in mind that there are those in our pews who are inwardly longing for a real, vital relationship with Christ and are in desperate need of good news.

Charles Spurgeon, the dynamic nineteenth-century minister, was once approached by a young preacher who complained that few people seemed to be converted in the services of his church. "You surely don't expect someone to be converted *every* Sunday?" asked Spurgeon. "Oh, no," answered the young man. "Then that's why no one is," Spurgeon concluded. Perhaps a little unfair, in the way of the elder clerics, but we preachers might get the point. After all, conversion is not necessarily a highly emotional once-and-for-all event. It is a turning from self to Christ which may take time and which needs to be constantly repeated. The great question is not, When was I converted? but, Am I converted? Am I, right now turned towards Christ, or have I let myself drift in other directions?

Evangelism within the churches should perhaps put more stress on the challenge to remain with Christ than on the call to come to him for the first time. Somehow we have fallen into the way of thinking that to preach the gospel must always mean appealing to a man or woman to forsake a consciously godless life and find salvation in Christ. But thousands today do not think of themselves as godless and therefore seem to have nothing spectacular to forsake. Among the millions in our cities there are few who are totally without any sense of God or experience of the church. So the gospel could be presented, not always in terms of Jesus' words "Come unto me," but in those other, deeply moving words that he spoke when the crowd was vanishing and the Cross loomed ahead: "Will you also go away?" If those who are on the fringe of our churches could hear that call and translate their *no* into a positive discipleship in a new and living relationship to Christ, what a transformation there would be in the field of evangelism! The world would know that the good news is real news and the churches are the nourishers and inspirers of living disciples.

From the churches then we turn to ourselves. Evangelism—who needs it? You need it. I need it. When we have examined all the reasons for our reluctance to be evangelists, don't we arrive in the end at the real truth: you and I are evangelists in proportion to the depth of our own loyalty to Christ. It is a hesitance about our own commitment that makes us unwilling to raise the question with anyone else. It is our faltering conviction and lack of trust that make us reluctant to communicate the faith. It is the poverty of our prayers, the indiscipline of our discipleship, the dimness of our vision that keep us from having something to declare. If, for some reason, Christ has ceased to mean very much in our lives, if he is not really central, then naturally we have nothing we feel important enough to pass on. We cease to be part of that life-giving stream that flows through the world from the presence of the living Christ.

Conversely, it is when we are close to the Lord himself, when we realize most vividly what he means in our lives, when we awake to the thought of what it would mean to us to try to live without him that we are irresistibly drawn to make him known. And that will then begin to happen in the most natural and simple ways, as well as in our support for the missionary enterprise of the church and sharing in the efforts of evangelism. In the end, it is a matter of what we really value most. There is nothing more natural than for us to share our enthusiasms. Everybody does it. We all have friends whose passion is for a certain brand of politics, a social cause, or a great reform. Others are devotees of opera, movies, railroads, or postage stamps. Whatever it is, their enthusiasm is infectious, and they show no reluctance in enlisting our interest in their cause or hobby. It is only the tired and cynical, the apathetic and bored, who have no such infectious zeal. Why then should it be considered strange, or in bad taste, if a Christian disciple wants to share what means more than anything else in the world? Why should we bottle up the most precious discovery we can possibly make? If we have responded to the call of Christ and found in him the way, the truth, and the life; if we are convinced that there is still more for us to discover about him and still more areas of discipleship to be explored; why should we not be instruments for passing on the news?

It should be stressed too that the over-arching loyalty we have to Christ by no means dims or slackens the other enthusiasms. Once when I had been doing some evangelizing in a prisoner-of-war camp where I happened to be detained along with some two hundred rather senior army officers, one of them who had experienced a Christian conversion said to me one day, "Now that I've become a Christian, I suppose I'll have to give up my great passion in life." Since I knew that this passion was for a country sport on which he had just written a book (that was published after the war) and not for drugs, or wife-beating, or fornication, I answered, "Why on earth? You'll probably get more fun out of it than ever." It takes a long time to persuade some people that the good news is about One who said, "I am come that they might have life, and have it more (not less) abundantly."

There is a great tide of new life coursing through this world. It flows from this Lord who was crucified for us and who calls on everyone to share in his new creation. You and I know of our need for this life, and if we have in any way experienced its cleansing and renewing power, must we not want to be instruments through which it flows? If we know anything of the salvation that Christ brings, do we not in a very vital sense have something to declare? I believe that the Spirit is moving among Christians today not just to reanimate our faith but to give it that infectious quality that is at the heart of evangelism. I believe that this same Spirit is not only awakening the spiritual life of the churches that are open to his power but is making them outgoing communities penetrating modern society with the Word and works of life. The good news is still something that everybody needs, and there is probably a particular area in which each of us can be effective. It is for us to find it, for the Lord is still saying to his entire church with all its members: "Go . . . and make disciples."